Edenderry, County Offaly, and the Downshire estate, 1790–1800

Maynooth Studies in Local History

SERIES EDITOR   Raymond Gillespie

This volume is one of five short books published in the Maynooth Studies in Local History series in 2007. Like their predecessors their aim is to explore aspects of the local experience of the Irish past. That local experience is not a simple chronicling of events that took place within a narrow set of administrative or geographically determined boundaries. Rather the local experience in the past encompasses all aspects of how local communities of people functioned from birth to death and from the pinnacle of the social order to its base. The study of the local past is as much about the recreation of mental worlds as about the reconstruction of physical ones. It tries to explore motives and meanings as well as the material context for people's beliefs. What held social groups together and what drove them apart are of equal interest and how consensus was achieved and differences managed can help to lay bare the lineaments of the local experience. The subject matter of these short books ranges widely. In the fraught world of the seventeenth century, in which religious division was endemic, communities in Cavan and Strabane managed to find enough common ground to make local worlds workable. Again in nineteenth-century County Dublin the desire for local improvement was sufficient to make the local government system triumph over political and religious division. Distress and division of another kind is evident in the emigration from nineteenth-century Ireland but the return of migrants with wealth and new experiences, an aspect of migration not much studied in the Irish context, helped to bind communities together again. Even in eighteenth-century Edenderry, on the Downshire estate, economic distress and political ferment in the 1790s strangely failed to produce military activity in the area in 1798. Understanding the common assumptions that held these communities together despite the tremendous pressures to which they were subjected is best done at the local level. Such communities remain the key to reconstructing how people, at many spatial and social levels, lived their lives in the past. Such research is at the forefront of Irish historical scholarship and these short books, together with the earlier titles in the series, represent some of the most innovative and exciting work being done in Irish history today. They provide models that others can use and adapt in their own studies of the local past. If these short books convey something of the enthusiasm and excitement that such studies can generate then they will have done their work well.

Maynooth Studies in Local History: Number 74

Edenderry, County Offaly,
and the Downshire estate
1790–1800

Ciarán Reilly

FOUR COURTS PRESS

Set in 10pt on 12pt Bembo by
Carrigboy Typesetting Services for
FOUR COURTS PRESS LTD
7 Malpas Street, Dublin 8, Ireland
e-mail: info@fourcourtspress.ie
http://www.fourcourtspress.ie
and in North America for
FOUR COURTS PRESS
c/o ISBS, 920 N.E. 58th Avenue, Suite 300, Portland, OR 97213.

ISBN 978–1–84682–061–8

Printed in Ireland
by ßetaprint, Dublin.

Contents

	Acknowledgments	5
	Introduction	7
1	Background to Edenderry in 1790	10
2	Social unrest, 1790–5	16
3	Defender disturbance and 'stirrings' of the French	21
4	Rebellion of 1798: Edenderry's part	31
5	Aftermath: courts martial and poverty	41
6	Conclusion: myth, legend and commemoration	46
	Appendix	51
	Notes	55

FIGURES

1	Taylor and Skinner, *Maps of the roads of Ireland*, 1783, showing Edenderry	11
2	Castro Petre church, Edenderry built in 1778	15
3	Sketch of Monasteroris House, Edenderry, the home of Nathaniel Preston, c.1785	17
4	Arthur Hills, 2nd marquis of Downshire, 1793–1801	19
5	Ballindoolin House, Carbury, Co. Kildare, attacked by Defenders from Edenderry in 1797	28
6	Celtic cross erected in 1874 over the grave of the Revd Mogue Kearns and Col. Anthony Perry hanged on Blundell Hill, 21 July 1798	37
7	President Sean T. O'Kelly and Cardinal Gilroy at Edenderry in 1950. The flag captured by George Brown at the battle of Foxes Hill, and known as the 'Whitechurch' flag is hanging behind them	47
8	Memorial stone unveiled in 1986 by Sean MacBride close to the spot where Kearns and Perry were hanged on Blundell Hill	48

Acknowledgments

I wish to thank a number of people who have made this publication possible. Firstly I am indebted to Dr C.J. Woods who supervised and offered excellent advice in the writing of the MA thesis on which this book is based. Similarly the opportunity that the series editor, Professor Raymond Gillespie, has provided me with by including my work in this year's series. For their assistance over the past few years during my research I offer many thanks to Professor R.V. Comerford, Mr Oliver Burke and Mr Padraig Foy. To the staff of the following institutions I am thankful for their co-operation and assistance: the National Library of Ireland; the National Archives of Ireland; the Deputy Keeper of the Public Records Office of Northern Ireland; the Russell and John Paul II libraries at NUI Maynooth; the Offaly County Library in Tullamore and the Edenderry Library. Finally I wish to thank Tara for her continued support, without which this work would not have been possible.

This work is dedicated to my parents, Mary and Tom, who have always encouraged me to pursue all of my dreams.

Introduction

This study examines the effects that the social, economic and political turmoil of the 1790s had on the Downshire estate at Edenderry in Co. Offaly, then known as King's County. The decline in fortunes of the woollen industry in Ireland towards the end of the 18th century had a catastrophic effect on Edenderry where upwards of a thousand people were employed in its production. The mismanagement of the estate, coupled with high rents and a shortage of basic provisions provided the radical Defender movement of the 1790s at Edenderry with a platform to emerge and wreak havoc on the estate. Having acquired the estate through marriage in 1786, Arthur Hill (later 2nd marquis of Downshire) paid very little attention to the declining fortunes of his estate in King's County. Despite being generally perceived to have escaped the attention of the United Irishmen and the 1798 rebellion, the county was heavily disturbed, and Edenderry and the surrounding Downshire estate was its most troubled area. In its location in the north east corner of the county, Edenderry was heavily affected by events outside the county border, in both Kildare and Meath.

Writing to Dublin Castle on 6 November 1796, the Revd William Lambart at Edenderry conveyed to the government in Dublin that it was the 'intention of the Defenders to rise on the seventeenth of this month, and to massacre the Protestants', and that he was 'in no doubt that the French would make a landing about this time'.[1] The vigilant Lambart had recently obtained this information after the arrest of Dennis Delaney, a United Irishman, and passed this and other discoveries to the administration at Dublin Castle. He was not alone in doing this, and with a constant contact with Dublin Castle, the letters of Shawe Cartland, William Lambart, Thomas Dames and John Everard provide us with an account of the daily occurrence of robberies and crimes at Edenderry. These letters, as well as the letters to the marquis of Downshire, show that there was an organized level of Defender and later United Irish activity at Edenderry in the 1790s.

The Rebellion papers in the National Archives, Dublin, in particular provide a remarkable insight into the period leading up to 1798, and the part played by the loyalists of the area in trying to curb the activities of the Defenders and United Irishmen. As early as 1795, the gatherings and crimes committed by the Defenders, aggrieved by social and agrarian issues, had come to the attention of the local magistrates who were worried at the support that existed in the Edenderry area for these conspirators. Similarly, the Downshire papers in the Public Record Office of Northern Ireland, shed light on Edenderry at this time, mainly through the correspondence of Downshire's agent, the erratic John Hatch. The unenviable job of overseeing the running of the marquis' estate at Edenderry (some 14,000 acres) fell to Hatch, and in his correspondence the social and economic condition of the estate is clearly outlined. However, the dwindling state of industry and decline in the town can be charted in these letters, and a picture emerges of instability and depression at Edenderry at this time.

Ruan O'Donnell has written about King's County in 1798, and has outlined the importance of the county when assessing 1798 in the midlands, which pre-1798 was the area which the government feared would pose most problems.[2] The fact that King's County was not a major theatre of operations does not mean that it was unaffected by the events of 1798, as O'Donnell claims. He points that it is possible that some of the rebels from the Edenderry area did play a part in events outside the county boundary. In his book, *Kildare in 98*, Pádraig Mac Suibhne states that King's County 'suffered badly in 1798 and that her history deserves to be written'.[3] Some historians have dealt with the rebellion of 1798 in county by county terms, and by doing so conclude that nothing of real significance happened in King's County. However, the rebellion transcended the county boundary, and it was in this way that Edenderry was heavily influenced by the distressed baronies of Carbury and Clonard. In his article on north Leinster in *1798: a bicentenary perspective*, Liam Chambers asks why rebellion did not happen in so many counties e.g. Queen's County, King's County and Westmeath.[4] Again, Edenderry falls into this category, as the area was heavily disturbed from 1795 to 1797 with the magistrates of the locality pleading with government for the district to be proclaimed.[5] One wonders then, why was there relative calm in the summer months of 1798 when rebellion eventually broke out.

The execution of the Revd Mogue Kearns and Colonel Anthony Perry in Edenderry on 21 July 1798, obviously was just reward for the loyal inhabitants of the town who had played such an important role of informing government and their landlord of the radical activities. Why was there such devoted loyalism in Edenderry and among its inhabitants? In his article 'King's County in 1798', Ruan O'Donnell states that there was an Orange Lodge in the 1790s at Edenderry. In fact, the town did not have one until 1824.[6] Instead, it was material interests and personal debt on the part of these loyalists that influenced the gentry around Edenderry. Similarly, when the actions of the Defenders are examined, it is clear that it was their response to social and agrarian issues that caused them to arm, more than a spirit of deep-rooted Republicanism emanating from the ideals of the French Revolution. The town was suffering greatly in the 1790s from the demise of the woollen industry, and the letters of Hatch and John Brownrigg to the marquis at Hillsborough outline the effects of what Hatch described as the 'drooping town',[7] in which famine, lack of provisions and rioting were common place.[8]

Like most local histories, the truth can get lost among the folklore and legends that exist. The town of Edenderry is not exempt from this, and most local tradition concerning the events leading up to and including 1798 is shrouded in myth. While agreeing that myth and legend mix well to make a good story, any undertaking of research should present the truth and show what actually transpired at the Downshire estate and its immediate vicinity in the period 1790–1800. While dispelling the myth and legend aspect of the rebellion, it is also instructive to examine how the locality celebrated the 1798 rebellion in 1898 and 1998. What is indeed peculiar is the veneration the Wexford rebels Kearns and Perry received, even though it was by chance that they came to be hanged at Edenderry. There was no commemoration of local heroes such as Captain Casey, hanged after a battle at Foxes Hill, or William Kennedy, hanged on Carbury Hill for his part in the attack on the Charter school at Carbury in 1797.

1. Background to Edenderry in 1790

Travelling on a tour through Ireland in 1780, Philip Luckombe noted that the town of Edenderry was a 'little inconsiderable place on the edge of the Bog of Allen'.[1] The town of Edenderry is located on the border of Offaly (King's County in the 1790s) and Kildare, close to the source of the river Boyne and at the edge of the great Bog of Allen, 65 kilometres from Dublin. In the 1790s Edenderry was the largest town in the barony of Coolestown, one of 12 baronies in King's County. Several other townlands such as Coneybury, Monasteroris and Kishawanna (which are all part of Edenderry today) were part of the Downshire estate at that time. It is important to bear in mind that they were all distinct villages in the 1790s.

The barony of Coolestown consisted of 48,000 acres, of which the marquis of Downshire of Hillsborough Castle, Co. Down, owned some 14,000 including the aforementioned villages as well as the town of Edenderry. The marquis' estate at Edenderry bordered on the counties of Kildare and Meath, a factor that had a major impact on the disturbances of the 1790s. The ownership of Edenderry passed into the hands of the marquis' family in 1786, when, Arthur Hill, the marquis' eldest son, Lord Kilwarlin, married Mary Sandys, heiress to Edenderry through her grandmother, a sister of Lord Blundell who had died in 1756. The marriage was seen as tactical on Arthur's part, a fact that made some in Hillsborough remark that 'her fortune is more than he wants or wished for, though it will do him no harm'.[2] She was one of the great heiresses of the day with £60,000 in ready money and £3,000 a year in other income. On the death of his father, Wills Hill, in 1793, Arthur became the 2nd marquis of Downshire, and with that the most powerful magnate of the late 18th century and the wealthiest landowner in Ulster. In total the Hill family owned 115,000 acres in Ireland and 5,000 in England, which included the elegant Easthampstead Park in Berkshire.

Arthur was powerful and enigmatic. During his brief reign at the head of the family (1793–1801) he was preoccupied with high politics and society in Britain as well as in Ireland, residing for the most part in Hanover Square, London. The Downshire estates in Ireland, which included Blessington in Co. Wicklow, Clonderlaw in Co. Clare and Hillsborough and Dundrum in Co. Down, were managed for the family by agents most of whom were absent from the estate. The lack of involvement in the southern estates ensured instability in the 1790s, and in Edenderry's case the incompetent

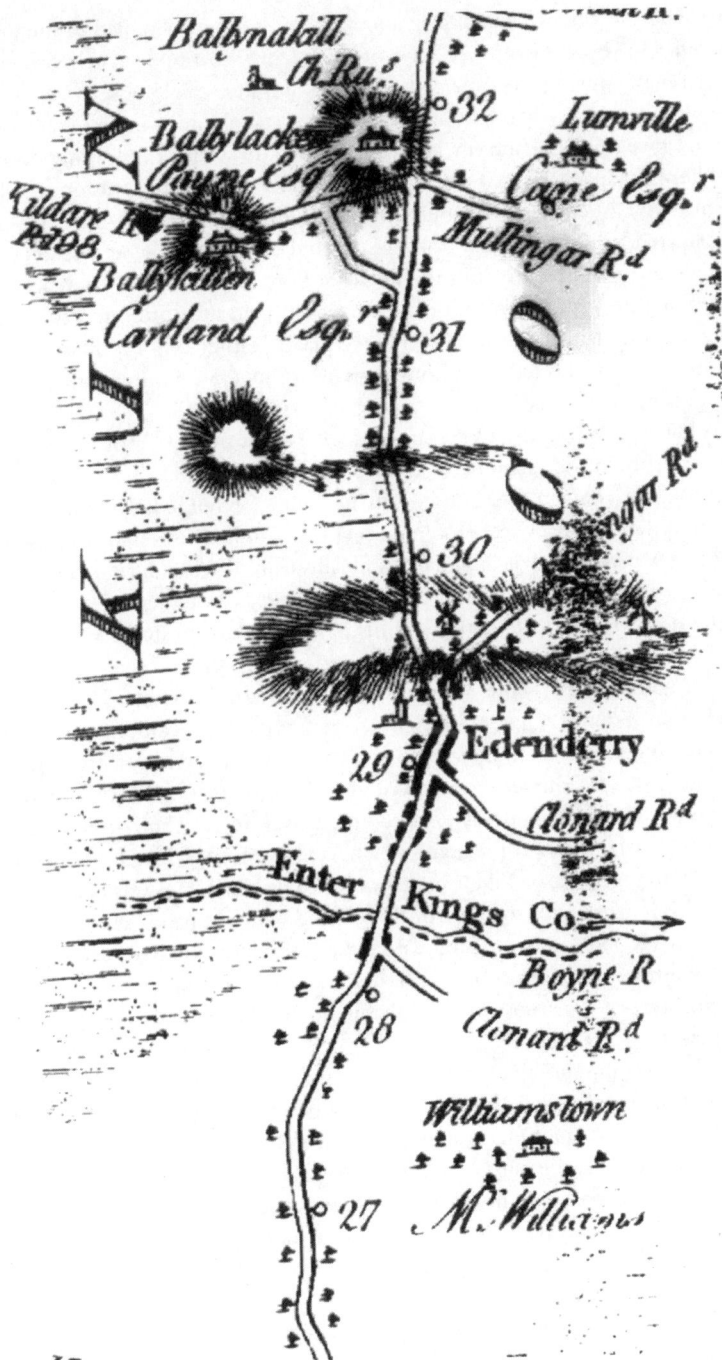

1 Taylor and Skinner, *Maps of the roads of Ireland*, 1783, showing Edenderry

John Hatch was left to run affairs, and for the most part he failed in the task at hand. However, Arthur was one of the regular correspondents with the government during this period, and his loyalty can be seen is such correspondence as when he stated that he was 'no alarmist, and an enemy of terror. I love my King and my country and will do what I think is my duty.'[3]

The mismanagement of the estate at Edenderry by Hatch was one of the reasons why a period of instability prevailed, during which time rents went uncollected and many of the holdings of land were out of lease. The decline of Edenderry had begun after the death of Lord Blundell in 1756, when his three daughters took control of the estate and paid little attention to affairs there, leaving it in the control of Henry Hatch, father of John. The transfer in ownership of the estate to Lord Downshire in 1786 did not improve the situation in Edenderry.

When examining the Downshire papers which survive from this period, caution should be exercised, as it appears that Hatch was a man of questionable character. On his death in 1797 it emerged that Hatch had incurred debts of over £20,000[4] and had even looked to resign his position in 1787, a proposal that angered Lord Kilwarlin.[5] The failure of Hatch to control the growing social and economic unrest at Edenderry led to much of the disturbances in the area, and his death in 1797 created a void, which left the town vulnerable in the summer months of 1798.

Throughout his tenure as agent for the Downshire estate, Hatch never resided in Edenderry, something that rendered his position even more difficult and which encouraged unlawful activity and later secret societies to operate. Many of the letters received at Hillsborough from Hatch mention his absence from Edenderry on account of severe weather or bad health, from which he suffered for many years. As early as 1781 Hatch commented that the town has 'for a long time past been dwindling' and was disillusioned to find Edenderry not thriving or flourishing which it had been in the years previous.[6] A petition of worsted weavers at Edenderry in 1810 mentions that an 'extensive trade' had been carried out in Edenderry some 40 years previously, and that most of the inhabitants had depended on the woollen business for their income.[7]

After visiting Edenderry in 1779, Hatch had noted that the woollen industry was in decline and that very few people if any were left employed in the business.[8] The Quaker community, which had been an integral part of the innovation and business at Edenderry, had quit the town and gone to Dublin on account of the decline in fortunes of their woollen industries. Among those who had gone to Dublin included John Wilson, Tom Bailey and 'Old Bewley'. According to Hatch, they had run into hard times and were now all bankrupt.[9]

There was a growing discontent among the inhabitants of Edenderry during the 1780s and despite the best efforts of Hatch who had put his own money into trying to revive the town, Edenderry was in his own words 'going down fast'.[10] The decline of the woollen industry resulted in riots and disturbances in the town, coupled with the 'high price of provisions' and a shortage of food.[11] In June 1783 Hatch relayed to Maria Blundell, daughter of Lord Blundell, that on his last visit to Edenderry 'there was not a potato or a grain of corn in the market'.[12] The rioting and disturbances led Hatch to replace the bailiff who he believed was not doing his job, and in 1784 it was a boast on his own part that there had not been a tree cut down or stolen in the previous year.[13]

Despite his shortcomings as an agent, Hatch did try his best to provide for the poor of Edenderry, and was helped in this endeavour by the generosity of the Blundell sisters, who did not want the people on their estate to go hungry.[14] However, their efforts were made difficult as most provisions available in Edenderry were 'monstrously dear',[15] and there was no corn, wool or black cattle at the local markets which had caused 'the mobs to riot'.[16] When the harvest was plentiful, Hatch was assured of visiting Edenderry where there was a 'certainty of peace'.[17] The last of those involved in the woollen trade at Edenderry was a man named Matt Hurst, whom Hatch was encouraging to remain. Hatch had given him money to employ the poor people of the area and also had endeavoured to have trees surrounding Blundell Castle cut down so as to provide timber for people to build cabins on their lands.[18]

The failure of Hatch to collect and return rents and tithes must have annoyed his employers during the 1780s and 90s. It seems that Hatch was reluctant to antagonize the locals because of their tendency to riot and cause disorder when the question of tithes and rents was raised. Even when times were relatively good there was a reluctance on the part of the inhabitants to pay, and Hatch claimed that the people were as 'liable to disturbance as any place' that he knew.[19] The estate lay destined to drift into ruin, and Hatch brought about several ejectments of tenants and claimed to Miss Blundell that the land might as well lie in waste in his own hands than in the hands of those who would not pay rent.[20]

Despite the decline of industry in the 1780s at Edenderry, there were signs of progress and development, which temporarily lifted the gloom surrounding the town. One such improvement was the Grand Canal passing close to Edenderry, which it was hoped would add to the value and prosperity of the estate. Writing about the canal in 1771, Charles Vallencey noted that the peasantry of Edenderry were starving and that 'nothing would contribute so much to their relief as an inland navigation'.[21]

Developing the Grand Canal through Edenderry occupied much of Hatch's time throughout his tenure as agent; indeed, he had a vested interest in the project as he had put much of his own finance in the venture.[22] He was adamant that it would bring about an economic turnaround at

Edenderry and pointed to nearby towns to which the canal had already passed through as proof that it would bring prosperity.[23] The matter was debated and later rebuffed in parliament, and Hatch believed it would be 'a very material point gained' if the canal succeeded in passing through the estate.[24] Writing to Miss Blundell, Hatch had assured her that the Grand Canal would be the 'making of Edenderry and your estate around it'.[25]

Occasionally Hatch ran into conflict with the Blundell sisters and later the Hills over the issue of the canal, as they were at times opposed to providing money for the building of the canal and had decided to 'not concern ourselves at all' with its building or progress.[26] It was a matter that annoyed Hatch, as he claimed he had never burdened the sisters for even 'a penny towards' the cost of the canal.[27] The canal would raise the spirits of the people who were suffering greatly from the decline of fortunes of the town, and Hatch was at pains to explain and convince the people of this.[28]

The distant location of Hillsborough meant that for the most part the marquis of Downshire was out of touch with the day-to-day affairs of his estate at Edenderry, and indeed it is questionable whether Edenderry concerned him much throughout this period. The collection of rents and tithes by Hatch was made difficult in the 1780s by the social and economic depression, which affected the area badly. However, some of the substantial landowners and middlemen were also reluctant and unable to pay what they owed to the estate. One such person was Shawe Cartland, who lived at the elegant Lumville House about four Irish miles from Edenderry.

As early as 1779, the debts of Cartland had come to the attention of the Blundell sisters and Hatch was trying his best to bring Cartland's affairs to some order, and had done much to find out about his general conduct. The task of collecting these rents from Cartland were made more difficult by the fact that he had been a magistrate for King's County since 1774. The debts incurred by Cartland played a major part in the affairs of the estate, amounting to over £4,000, and if Hatch could not get Cartland to pay, he had little hope of getting money from the small leaseholders. This was one of the reasons why Kilwarlin had objected to Hatch's resignation as agent in 1787.[29] On account of these debts owed to the estate, Hatch informed Miss Blundell in March 1782 that he had told Cartland that he no longer considered him as a friend and was taking the necessary steps to recover the 'monstrous arrear' that was due by him. Cartland responded by admitting that he was entirely in the wrong and was at Hatch's mercy, and stated that he was willing to sell all his stock to reduce the debt.

The exertions of Cartland, who was very active in apprehending Defenders and United Irishmen, was his way of trying to appease the marquis who was anxious for him to pay the debt he owed to the estate. He was also an informant of Dublin Castle, receiving large sums of money from the Secret Service fund.[30] The loyalty of Cartland can be questioned in light

2 Castro Petre church, Edenderry built in 1778

of his financial debt, as it seems he was more concerned with maintaining his position within the elite in Edenderry and avoiding the issue of paying what he owed to the estate.

In late 1789 Hatch finally persuaded Lord Kilwarlin, after three years, to visit Edenderry. Owing to a preoccupation with events in Co. Down and with a heated election in 1790, Kilwarlin showed little interest in affairs at Edenderry. The erratic Hatch, who had ulterior motives for the development of Edenderry, was left with the task of administering the estate despite his ill- health. Several instances had occurred in the 1780s to suggest that conspirators and elements of society at Edenderry were unhappy with those in authority. The newly built Protestant church was damaged on various occasions and copper stolen from the roof.[31] In October 1786, *The Times* reported that five local men were whipped after being found guilty at the assizes for administering unlawful Whiteboy oaths.[31] The simmering discontent of the inhabitants of Edenderry and its surrounding area would soon boil over in the 1790s.

2. Social unrest, 1790-5

In August 1792, John Pomeroy, son of Lord Harberton, wrote from the elegant Palladian mansion at Newbury Hall, six kilometres from Edenderry, that the Catholics of the country were pressing their claims in an impudent and barefaced manner and that in general the 'people's minds were very uneasy'.[1] The economic repercussions from the decline of the woollen industry continued to have a major effect on the nearby Downshire estate in the early years of the 1790s.

Conditions at Edenderry were temporarily relieved by the generosity of Miss Blundell who gave £50 for the relief of the poor in 1793.[2] The tenants on the estate were, in Hatch's words 'in a dismal way from the want of turf, which they could not get home from the bog on account of the dismal wet season we have had'.[3] As was the case in several other parts of the country, the activities of Whiteboys and Defenders were beginning to take root as a result of this social unrest. According to Thomas Bartlett, King's County was heavily disturbed by the Militia riots of 1793 and also by the Defender disturbances in the early part of the decade.[4] In his memoirs of the rebellion Sir Richard Musgrave claimed that one radical secret society, the Defenders, in King's County were 'the best organized in the kingdom'.[5]

There were however, some encouraging signs for improvement at Edenderry in the early 1790s, despite Hatch's reluctance to perform his duties as agent. The returns of the Kildare Lent assizes in 1792 show that several different people at Edenderry were granted money to carry out repairs to the roadways leading from the town into the county of Kildare. The sum of £24 was given to Patrick Connor and William Grattan of Williamstown House, to repair the road from Edenderry to Johnstown.[6] The new road from Carrick Hill to the river Boyne was to be repaired by Daniel Jackson and Patrick Reilly, as was the road from Edenderry to the bridge at Clonard.[7] Similar road improvements are mentioned in a letter from Hatch to Lord Downshire in 1790, when he refers to a Nicholas Crawford looking to carry out repairs so that trade between Tullamore and Edenderry could be improved.[8] There were also plans made by Hatch in 1791 for the provision of a school and the building of a market house. However, like most of Hatch's plans, neither of these came to fruition, the market house was not built until 1826 under the 3rd marquis, and the school in 1801 was described as being in need of much repair.

3 Sketch of Monasteroris House, Edenderry, the home of
Nathaniel Preston, *c.*1785

Other instances of improvements at the estate throw light on the growing
social unrest, which was developing at Edenderry. The recently built Protestant
church, Castro Petre, had been targeted by Defenders, who stole copper
from the roof of the building for a second time.[9] Money which had been
provided to make a footpath to the church was used instead for 'lattice wire
to defend the windows'.[10] The work carried out in 1789 and 1790 by the men
of a Mr Harman, who had quarried stones for the re-roofing of the church,
was undone in January 1791, when more damage to the church was reported.[11]

The visit of Lord Kilwarlin to the estate in April 1789 had raised hopes
for the improvement of life and conditions at Edenderry.[12] However, the
'heated' elections of 1790 in Co. Down and a law suit against a tenant at the
Dundrum estate preoccupied Hillsborough in the early years of the 1790s.
The 1790 election had caused him to waste 'about thirty thousand pounds
and lead a most uncomfortable life for about six to eight months', which
when compared with the expenditure of the 1783 election (£3,000) shows
the rivalry that existed between the Hills and the Stewarts.[13] His appoint-
ment in 1793 to the privy council meant that even less time was devoted to
the management of his estates.

The law suit against the tenant John McCartney preoccupied Hatch also,
as the case dragged on for nearly four years from 1788 to 1792. It is interesting

to note that Shawe Cartland owed the marquis a similar debt at Edenderry but was never brought before the court and held accountable. The clever Cartland found other means to win favours at Hillsborough; these usually involved apprehending Defenders and informing his lordship of the minds of his fellow gentry on the estate at Edenderry. As a magistrate and as a lieutenant of the yeomanry, Cartland used all his influence to cover up his debt.

The Grand Canal was progressing steadily through the countryside, and had passed by the town as early as 1793 when Shawe Cartland had a bridge named in his honour close to his lands at Lumville.[14] Along with his brother George, who was ironically employed at this time as a commissioner of bankruptcy in the Court of Chancery, Shawe had invested almost £300 in the Grand Canal venture. The canal had also made enough progress for passage boats to reach Philipstown in May 1796.[15] However, the cut of the canal to the town of Edenderry, which Hatch had campaigned for, was not added until 1804 after considerable difficulty as much of its course was through bog. The estate at Edenderry was 'economically depressed' according to W.A. Maguire,[16] and all Hatch could hope for was that the town would 'mend with the times, which are at present very sad'.[17] The relief provided by the Blundells in 1792 and 1793, did help to relieve the poor, who must have been quite numerous as Hatch's nephew was making a list of the poor for him so that he could apportion the Blundells 'most worthy donation in the most proper way'.[18]

Hatch spent little time at the estate in the early 1790s, again ill health and the weather were the most common excuses for poor returns of rents and leases. There were long periods of time when Hatch did not write at all to Hillsborough or to Miss Blundell. In January 1794 he made returns of £1,300 for the estate, but no correspondence survives until early August of that year, when he hoped to 'complete the returns soon'.[19] In January 1795 Miss Blundell was urging Hatch to complete his returns for Edenderry, which had been 'a sort of distress to us to be so long without them'.[20] It is easy to lay the blame for most of the inefficiency of the estate with Hatch, but there was growing discontent among the inhabitants of the estate who refused to pay rents to an absentee landlord. Their frustrations would soon boil over, and were inflicted upon the gentry in the 'big houses' surrounding the estate.

The social and economic crisis, which was experienced by most of the inhabitants of the Downshire estate at Edenderry, had culminated in rising prices, unemployment and ejectments from holdings as rents and tithes could not be paid. This in turn created an environment which allowed the emergence of secret societies such as the Defenders who began to cause havoc on the estate. There is no evidence to suggest that the ideals of the United Irishmen had permeated through to the estate, although there was a branch in Tullamore as early as 1793.[21]

4 Arthur Hills, 2nd marquis of Downshire, 1793–1801

By July 1795, there was a growing sense of fear among the law abiding community at Edenderry, who wrote to Lord Downshire asking for help in defending their homes and the estate from the increasing Defender mayhem. Writing from Dublin Castle, Lord Camden assured Downshire that General Craig was in a position to deploy sufficient forces to satisfy the people of Edenderry.[22] Further proof that the situation at Edenderry was deteriorating can be seen in a letter from Sir Fenton Aylmer, high sheriff of Kildare, to Downshire in November 1795, asking him for a £10 subscription to the Kildare Association for preserving the peace, as Downshire's lands bordered with Co. Kildare which was quite a troubled area.[23]

The location of Edenderry was, in the 1790s, considered of strategic importance to the safety and defence of the realm, as it was located close to the main Dublin to Galway roadway and it was in close proximity to the disturbed counties of Kildare and Meath.[24] The importance of the town was seen in 1795 when Henry Keating proposed that the town be one of five defensive cordons to protect the capital. The defensive cordon of 50 Irish miles would be protected by an army garrison at or near to Edenderry.[25] A key reason why the town would remain relatively calm when rebellion broke out in the summer of 1798 was the stationing of these troops in Edenderry. The location of so many gentry houses in and around the Downshire estate, such as Lumville, Rahan and Ballyburley, made them easy prey for the disgruntled Defenders who in 1795 began to raid their homes for arms, money and foodstuffs. In all there were 18 gentry houses, seven of which were located within the Downshire estate, the remainder within five miles of Edenderry in the baronies of Warrenstown and Carbury. It was, as we shall see in the next chapter, these gentry many of whom were magistrates for King's County, who wrote to Dublin Castle and Hillsborough trying to have the area proclaimed to be in a state of rebellion.

The courts martial which followed in the wake of the 1798 rebellion provide remarkable evidence as to the activities and working of the Defender movement at Edenderry throughout the 1790s. The case of Edward Allen and Michael Costello in February 1800 is one such trial, where the Defender plot to murder John Wakely, a local magistrate and justice of the peace comes to light. As early as 1795 Wakely had become a prime target for the Defenders who planned to raid his home at Ballyburley House and murder him. The Defenders were a well-organized body and had in their ranks several captains, a court for trying people guilty of crime and a grand jury to decide the outcome of such events. At the trial of Allen and Costello in 1800, the outcome of one such Defender court was relayed to the assizes when William Welsh and Patrick De Bor were charged with having struck Frank Gore, and were duly summonsed to trial in Anthony Kennedy's bog.[26] Now calling themselves 'true born Frenchmen', the Defender conspiracy was gathering pace and 1796 would prove how well organized they were and how disaffected they had become.

3. Defender disturbance and 'stirrings' of the French

The Defender conspiracy was rapidly gathering pace, and by 1796 the inhabitants of the Downshire estate, lived in fear of the almost daily threat of robberies and outrages. The magistrates of the barony of Coolestown and Warrenstown met in August 1796, and were adamant that 'a strong military force is indispensably necessary' for the area.[1] The magistrates had previously made an appeal to the government in 1795 for a military force to be stationed at Edenderry, which they hoped would prevent the spread of Defenderism, which was developing all around them.

The Drogheda Militia, which had been stationed at Edenderry, had left by the summer of 1796 because they had been badly accommodated in the town,[2] and Cartland was sorry to inform Dublin Castle 'that we never had more cause to apprehend the breaking out of disturbance than we have at present'.[3] Anger was expressed by Cartland that the Drogheda Militia had been sent to Portarlington a town where 'Defenderism had never made the smallest appearance'.[4] Three deserters from this regiment had been arrested by Cartland, namely Thomas Cassidy, Robert Carney and John Hamilton. In the nearby village of Rhode in the barony of Warrenstown, a man had been murdered for refusing to take the Defender oath. The deep-rooted nature of the Defender society was evident at the subsequent assizes, when no approvers could be found to testify against the culprits.[5]

The local gentry were dismayed as to what course of action to take to curb the threat of Defenders, who it was reported, went about at night in large bodies taking arms and carrying fire to torch the thatched houses, and were swearing into their society both men and women. The recently built Grand Canal was also a target for the Defenders who were plundering boats bringing goods to and from Dublin. The Canal Company formed its own yeomanry corps of canal employees around Edenderry to 'suppress Defenderism and preserve the public peace'.[6] A blunderbuss and a case of pistols were purchased for the safety of each passage boat travelling the Grand Canal. At Downshire's insistence, the magistrates and gentry formed themselves into a yeomanry corp in October 1796, consisting of the gentlemen of the baronies of Coolestown and Warrenstown. The local gentry had previously in 1777 formed a unit of volunteers, to defend the country as the country was left vulnerable during the American War of Independence. In 1796 they maintained their colours of scarlet and black for their yeomanry corps. This consisted of 42 volunteers, with John Wakely of Ballyburley as captain, Thomas Dames of Greenhills as a lieutenant and Charles Palmer Esq. of Rahan also as an officer. The need for such a corps was reflected in Revd George Lambart's letter to Downshire in the wake of a series of house and highway robberies in late September 1796. The yeomanry corps, he wrote, 'goes on with some spirit, the subscriptions amount already to seven hundred guineas'.[7] The corps was overwhelmingly Protestant, and the registrar of the corps, John Everard, had only included one 'poor' Catholic man because 'Mr Pelham's speech in parliament removed the idea of making any objections to them'.[8] One can detect a certain sectarian element in the attitude of the yeomen, who felt that in the boggy terrain of the Downshire estate, where a horse could not act, the 'fool', as the Catholic man was referred to as, could do a good job instead.

Alarmingly for the magistrates of the barony (11 in number), the Defenders at Edenderry were without doubt familiar at this stage with the ideals of the United Irishmen as they were reported to be calling themselves the 'French Militia'[9] and 'true born Frenchmen'.[10] Having established themselves, the Defenders now met in large numbers where weapons instructions were carried out, such as occurred on 2 October 1796, when 300 Defenders assembled and were addressed by 'a gentleman from the Co. Westmeath'.[11] It was also stated by Lambart that some of their own society were tried at these meetings and if found guilty were shot dead and buried on the spot. According to Lambart the Defenders were firmly anti-Protestant and were sworn in to 'assist in the murdering of all Protestants'.[12] These 'true born Frenchmen' were however, strictly forbidden to rough cattle, burn houses or steal (except arms) until they received orders from their captains. The capture of Dennis Delaney in September 1796 by Lambart produced evidence that the Defenders at Edenderry had adopted the ideals of the United Irishmen. A deserter from the Queen's County Militia, Delaney was arrested and found to have in his possession the resolutions of the United Irishmen, a rebellious song against 'King and constitution' and secret oaths of admission. The sectarian nature and intentions of the Defenders and United Irishmen can be seen in a verse that was found in the possession of Delaney at Edenderry, which contained the lines 'we'll burn houses and break doors, we'll kiss the ministers daughters and make them whores, the Papists few we'll make them rue, when Johnny gives us warning'.[13]

The papers found on Delaney also contained the initials HJMcC, which Lambart reported to Pelham at Dublin Castle were those of Henry Joy McCracken, one of four brothers from Antrim involved in 'the United Irishmen and in assassination'.[14] The mission of Delaney was obviously sanctioned from the Belfast Society of United Irishmen, who were anxious to spread their ideals throughout the country. In his correspondence with

Dublin Castle, Lambart also claimed that another paper found on Delaney involved sanctioning the murder of two men belonging to the Fifeshire regiment, who Delaney and Butler were to 'take vengeance on in the true republican style'.[15] The magistrates had established a system of informers at Edenderry who had infiltrated the Defender ranks, but they were at odds as to what powers they had to disperse Defender gatherings. The Defenders at the Downshire estate it seems were awaiting a landing of the French, which they were 'in no doubt of' arriving and it was then intended to 'massacre the Protestants'.[16] That Theobald Wolfe Tone's expedition did not leave France until December 1796 shows that that the Defenders at Edenderry had some knowledge of the plans of the United Irishmen. They had also recruited into their ranks disaffected members of the militia stationed at Edenderry.

The situation had deteriorated over the winter months, when the cover of darkness gave the Defenders an opportunity to strike; this is obvious in the increase of letters sent to Dublin Castle from Edenderry in 1797. The Revd Lambart suggested that the magistrates should 'take up' these Defenders who had been involved in stealing arms and send them to Dublin, so that the government could deal with them as they wished. This, Lambart perceived, would be a less reactive measure than having the area proclaimed.[17] He was not alone in his sentiments when Thomas Knipe wrote from Castlerickard in Co. Meath describing the 'very disturbed state of that part of Meath that joins the King's County' and the actions of the 'French Militia' who marched into the King's County. According to Knipe the 'French Militia' made a distinction between Protestant and Papist, the latter he claimed they only robbed but the former 'they endeavour to murder and in some instances they have unfortunately succeeded'.[18]

The day-to-day affairs of the estate did not improve and Hatch claimed to Miss Blundell that 'the disturbed state of the country and the advantage taken thereof by bad people' made it difficult for him to bring the accounts to order.[19] The debt incurred by Cartland was still unresolved, and in January 1796 Hatch was asking Downshire's advice on whether he should eject Cartland from his lands.[20] There were attempts by Quaker businessmen to try and revive the town of Edenderry, but Downshire, who was always suspicious of the Quakers, rejected these.[21] The town with its dilapidated buildings could not provide an adequate barrack for the military[22] and the yeomanry were badly equipped and were requesting new equipment, uniforms and horses.[23] The marquis was informed in February 1797 that the Defenders were 'playing the devil at Edenderry', the murder of Isaac Bagnall of Tubberdaly on 8 February being proof of this.[24] The murder of Bagnall and his wife Sarah was particularly violent and showed that 'old scores' were being settled by the Defenders. Prior to the murder of the Bagnalls, there had been numerous house robberies, attested with 'great instances of cruelty' and an 'eagerness to carry off firearms' by the Defenders.[25] Bagnall was described as being an 'honest industrious Protestant' who lived adjoining the estate at Clonlack.

The trial of Thomas Maypowder and Henry Proctor from Edenderry in September 1797 outlined the cruelty with which the Bagnalls had met their end. The youngest of the Bagnalls, Mary, who while staying at Edenderry with relatives identified two of her parent's 'assassins'. The Defenders demanded arms and threatened to burn down the house, which they duly did. They also looked for money, which Sarah Bagnall kept in a box, which shows that the perpetrators were familiar with the household. Having recovered from being shot in the chin, John Bagnall recalled being shot at as he dragged his parents from the burning house. Having murdered Isaac, some of the Defenders were heard to shout that he would not 'go tory hunting anymore'. More than 27 men were arrested for their part in the attack including one Pender from Edenderry, but only Maypowder and Proctor stood trial.[26] As was the case with several Defender trials, the accused received several good character references and were acquitted of the murder, despite the pleas of Lambart and Dames.[27]

The magistrates and yeomanry, having tried 'every exertion' but 'without effect', could see no other option than having the barony proclaimed to be in a state of disturbance, this they hoped would eventually quell Defender activities.[28] Having met at Edenderry in April 1797, the magistrates wrote individual letters to Dublin Castle to outline the situation that existed in the barony. Prior to their meeting in April, three members of the Coolestown yeomanry had been robbed of their arms and their houses plundered. As many of the yeomanry had many miles to ride home from parading in Edenderry, they would be rendered useless by depositing their arms in a depot, as was suggested by officials in Dublin Castle. According to John Everard, if the yeomen were unarmed they would be exposed to the 'malevolence of the common people'.[29] Writing from Beauparc in Navan, the Rev George Lambart noted that 'in Clonard and Edenderry the principles' of the Defenders 'are carried with most general success'.[30] The nightly patrols of yeomanry had failed to lift any of these Defenders, who in June 'attacked and carried away arms from a house near Edenderry during divine service'.[31] Another daring attempt was made by the Defenders, who in May, attacked the gaol of Philipstown to secure the release of prisoners but were repulsed.[32]

The failure of the assizes to prosecute Defenders increased the sense of fear among the Protestant landowners who were the victims of many of the Defender attacks. Some of the informers had been threatened by Defenders. One was Francis Carey, who was held at knifepoint and made swear that he would be 'true to the French when they landed' and that he would assist in the coming revolution.[33] As a result of these actions and 'thro bribery', the approvers that had been gathered for the spring assizes had denied everything that they had previously sworn to the magistrates.[34]

The ever-vigilant Lambart concluded that on account of the seizure of arms by the Defenders, their numbers would increase and t their 'actions would become more desperate and more general' and that very soon the towns would fall sacrifice to the Defenders as had the houses in the countryside.[35] In April 1797, Lambart proposed, although acknowledging it a severe measure, that 'all suspected homes should be examined at night, and where the men were not found home, if they could not the next day show in a satisfactory manner where they had been, to burn the houses'.[36] That such a measure was necessary can be seen in the comments of Alex Kerr, a farmer close to Carbury village and John Pomeroy. In May, John Pomeroy commented on the 'rebellious disposition that now prevails among the idle and lower classes of people',[37] while Kerr noted that in recent weeks 'hundreds of men had gone about the country under the pretence of selling potatoes' but were singing republican songs.[38]

The issuing of an oath of allegiance by Dublin Castle it seems was a measure designed to ease the minds of the magistrates and gentry who failed to have the barony proclaimed, despite the nearby barony of Carbury in Co. Kildare being proclaimed in May 1797. The oath of allegiance was 'for the use of those deluded people who surrender themselves before 24 May'.[39] The Revd Lambart, as ever eager to win the favour of those in Dublin Castle, requested 500 copies of the oath, which he believed was a 'pleasing demand'.[40] Another who wrote to Dublin Castle of the necessity of proclaiming the area was Mr Nelson of Monasteroris who also believed that nothing but 'nightly patrols will effectively break this alarming and diabolical threat to our lives and property',[41] while Everard maintained that he was exposed to the malevolence of his misguided neighbours'. Having witnessed the attack on Mr White, a Quaker at Monasteroris, who shot a Defender dead during the attack, Everard informed Dublin Castle that White was prepared to let a house for the provision of extra troops to be stationed there. As a measure to promote stricter discipline among the ranks of the militia, White also agreed to furnish the soldiers with meat, which would mean that they would have no reason to 'straggle about Edenderry market or have any intercourse with the common people'.[42]

An attack on the Charter school at Carbury on the night of 6 May 1797 prompted the magistrates of Co. Kildare to proclaim the barony of Carbury. Consisting of over 200 men, the Defenders many of whom were from Edenderry, attacked the house for over an hour. According to Lambart, they were unable to carry off their dead.[43] The master of the school, Stephen Sparks, as sergeant of the Carbury yeomanry was an obvious target for the Defenders; as he was also believed to be a spy.[44] On the night of the attack Sparks had noticed that the Defenders assembled on the Hill of Carbury and showed a 'great appearance of regularity'.[45] Having sent a dispatch to Edenderry for help, Sparks was left to defend the school with his 15-year-old son, James

and nine men who included Mr Samuels, Arthur Smith, John Jackson and
Gilbert Walker. The Revd Lambart had received information on the same
day that Edenderry was to be attacked and 'every precaution was taken to
secure the place and the night ended in a disappointment', which suggests
that Lambart and others were prepared to give battle.[46] The fighting began
at Sparks' house around midnight when the Defenders broke the windows
of the house with stones and there continued 'a constant heavy fire kept up
on both sides for about an hour and a quarter'. The Wicklow militia under
Lieutenant Hempenstall came to their assistance having proceeded from
Edenderry to give assistance to Richard Grattan Esq. of Williamstown,
whose house was also threatened on the same night as he was deemed to be
'highly obnoxious to the Defenders'.[47] Hempenstall later claimed that the
firing of muskets could be heard in Edenderry.[48]

The arrival of the militia managed to disperse the Defenders, but the
militia suffered a casualty when one of their party was shot dead by Sparks'
men, who had mistaken him for a Defender. In Sparks' estimation there
were at least six rebel dead and many more wounded. One Defender who
was captured was later executed, although Chambers states that many men
were executed for their part in the attack.[49] Other Defenders were apprehended at Temple Jude, which had been a place of rendezvous, trying to
conceal and bury those killed in the attack. The Wicklow Militia were happy
to have 'done their duty' and published an address stating such.[50] Prior to
this a circular had appeared in Edenderry praising the 'zeal and spirit' of the
Wicklow Militia.

In the search that followed the attack, the Wicklow Militia arrested
Stephen Hyland and William Kennedy, the former offering to act as an
approver and testify against the Defenders if his life was spared. The trial of
William Kennedy in Athy on 24 August 1797, showed how anxious the
magistrates were to have him convicted, as one of the jurors was threatened
with been thrown out the window if he did not find Kennedy guilty.[51]
Despite the case being referred to the lord lieutenant, Kennedy was hanged
at the spot, where he had been 'heard to say that he would plant the tree of
liberty'.[52] Although having supplied several names to the magistrates, which
included Defenders from Edenderry such as James Casey of Coneyburrow a
canal worker, James Walsh and Edward Ryan,[53] Hyland was sentenced to
death by the court in which he testified against Kennedy after he had
secured the imprisonment of eight others who were lodged in Naas gaol.[54]

The case of William Kennedy of Kishawanna continued to be a major
talking point at Edenderry after his execution. However the surveyor of the
Canal Company and later agent to the marquis of Downshire, John
Brownrigg, sheds light on the prisoner Kennedy of whom many people
'spoke favourably'. Kennedy, he claimed, had allowed himself to become
involved in the 'popish mania that is of late spiralling itself amongst the

lower classes' who were now calling themselves 'the Rosary or Scapular of the Blessed Lady'. It also appeared that Kennedy had applied on the day of the attack to buy gunpowder from two Quaker shopkeepers, William Bailey and Joseph Barnes.[55] However, despite Barnes' statement to Brownrigg, which described Kennedy as 'punctuated and honest in his dealings', this information did not appear at the trial because as a Quaker, Barnes would not give evidence under oath.[56]

Evidence given at the trial of Kennedy suggests that he may have been intoxicated on the night of the attack on the Charter school and thus incapable of carrying out any involvement with the Defenders. Giving evidence for the prisoner, Patrick Reilly stated that he had met with Kennedy in Edenderry on the night of the attack and found him so drunk that he would not give him the 15 shillings he owed him for shoes. Later in the evening Reilly claimed that they both drank in Duff's ale house in Kishawanna, a claim that was reiterated by Catherine Duff. According to Duff, Kennedy was the 'drunkest man she had ever saw' and he quarrelled with her when she refused him more ale. Fearing the wrath of the soldiers she did not let him stay any longer and said that he made for home, which was just five or six perches from her house. Another witness called before the court was Rose Kennedy of New Chapel whom it was claimed the prisoner was courting at the time. Appearing 'a modest and beautiful girl', she told the court that Kennedy 'was so drunk he was hardly able to walk', and that when she heard the shots from Carbury Hill she sent him on his way, apparently fearing her father who would be angry if he knew of Kennedy's presence there. *The Press* newspaper reporting the trial commented that it took the jury over eighteen and half hours to deliver there verdict of guilty which indicates that there may have been some truth in the evidence given before the court.[57]

Although the attack on the Charter school had ended in disaster for the Defenders, their spirit and enthusiasm was not easily quashed, as a subsequent attack on the home of John Purdon of Ballindoolin made clear. On 16 May 1797, a 'banditti' of over 300 men mostly on horseback armed with guns and swords (which suggests that they were prosperous) made off with over £200 after making Purdon 'swear six or seven Defender oaths'. Among the items taken from Purdon's home were whiskey, knives, cloth and delft, which indicates a non-political motive on the part of the Defenders. The home of Patrick De Bor was also threatened, but having heard the shots fired at Purdon's home, the De Bors (a family of Dutch origin and originally timber merchants) were armed and the Defenders made off without success.[58]

The Quaker community in general were not a target of the Defenders, although some of their members had arms stolen from them. The Quakers believed, as was pointed out to Francis Metcalf, that their members should not 'place confidence in the arm of the flesh' or have any involvement with

5 Ballindoolin House, Carbury, Co. Kildare, attacked by
Defenders from Edenderry in 1797.

the military. In 1797 the society at Edenderry were remiss about the matter
of arms, according to the quarterly meeting that was held in the town. The
form of punishment that a Quaker received for possessing arms was to be
disunited, as was Henry Clibborn who refused to meet with the society.[59]
The home of Francis Metcalf was attacked in November 1797 by a group of
armed men who stole his gun. Visiting Quakers noted that in the wake of
the attack, Metcalf had secured the services of two soldiers for his protection. This, he was told, was in 'gross violation of the peaceable testimony we
as a people hold forth to the world'. Others such as Francis Milner claimed
he had destroyed his gun, while Thomas Neale claimed that, as a Freeman of
Cork City, he was entitled to carry a gun for his own protection.[60]

The lack of a resident landlord or agent at the estate at Edenderry must
have frustrated the local magistrates. While doing their best to foil the
Defender conspiracy, they (Cartland claimed), 'remained base to be easily
murdered' in their homes.[61] The volatile situation at Edenderry was not
helped by John Hatch's failure to find a replacement bailiff after Joseph
Wilson had died in 1796. The death of Hatch himself was reported to the
marquis on 23 September 1797, and his son-in-law, Francis Synge was left
with the task of sorting out Hatch's financial and estate papers, which were,
in a state of disarray.[62] At the time of Hatch's death the arrears at the estate
amounted to £9,361 and some tenants had not paid rent since 1783. One of
the last jobs carried out by Hatch had been to compile the rental of the

estate, which showed that Cartland owed more than £1,000 and that he had not surveyed any of his lands for quite some time.[63] Francis Synge commented that Hatch had been 'much too compassionate for the office of agent' and that it would have been better for the both parties had he been allowed to resign his position some 20 years earlier.[64]

The yeomanry corps did have some success in 1797. By the end of the year they had managed to secure extra troops to the area, which included the Wicklow Militia and the Royal Artillery. The Wicklow Militia under Captain Hempenstall were stationed at Edenderry and in the summer of 1797 they inflicted heavy damage on houses of suspected rebels in Co. Westmeath.[65] Why this measure was not adopted in the barony of Coolestown where the militia were surrounded by Defenders is interesting. The infantry at Edenderry in March 1797 were praised by Thomas Pelham for their 'zealous and loyal exertions'.[66] Other successes for the yeomanry against the Defenders were reported in July when Lambart commented that a number of 'idle and disorderly fellows' who while placed in gaol had resulted in Edenderry becoming 'quiet and robberies ceased about this time'.[67] However, since they were released from gaol, Lambart noted that they were high in the spirit that 'the French will be here in less than three weeks'.[68] In May 1797, Cartland was happy to report to Dublin Castle that the Wicklow Militia had shot one robber dead, another had been wounded at Carbury and brought to Edenderry, and the Rathangan yeomanry apprehended two Defenders close to Edenderry. A further arrest of a man carrying a cart of gunpowder through Edenderry was a major success for the yeomanry. During divine service at Castro Petre, Cartland had been called from church, as this man produced an old licence for carrying gunpowder. An angry mob who would 'probably rescued him' had the yeomanry not arrived descended upon Cartland as he arrested him. The capture of Defenders and 'villains' continued as the conspirators fled in great numbers and the magistrates were in pursuit of more of them.[69] To increase further the safety of the barony, Cartland proposed that a military guard be placed at the home of every magistrate who was the prime target of the Defenders.[70] Some of the magistrates feared that their fellow justices of the peace might become disillusioned if the Defenders continued to roam the countryside. The government were thus encouraged to act with energy on the matter to prevent a sense of 'listlessness' creeping in among the magistrates.[71]

Despite the success of the yeomanry in apprehending Defenders and the stationing of the military at Edenderry, the threat of Defenders and United Irishmen loomed large at the Downshire estate as 1797 came to a close. In September, William Evans, barrack master on the Grand Canal, wrote of the large gatherings of Defenders at Edenderry and that despite stern measures the attacks on houses for arms and money continued.[72] The high sheriff of King's County, Thomas Dames, was convinced that the gentlemen would quit their country homes once the winter set in, and that this would create further anarchy and dismay.[73] Problems of law and order of a different kind emerged when Dames had to abandon a meeting of the magistrates in Birr because members of the militia were present and not entitled to vote.[74]

Following the summer assizes at Philipstown, John Pollock, clerk of the crown for Leinster, wrote that in his opinion their existed an 'unequivocal determination 'to subvert the King's government', another attempt to prosecute Defenders having failed.[75] A visiting judge, Robert Day, also commented that the gentlemen of the surrounding baronies had barricaded their homes and had no intention of abandoning their 'defensive system or relaxing their precautions till after the winter'.[76] Without a military presence in the area, Pollock informed Dublin Castle, the consequences of the coming winter could be disastrous. The military, he claimed, by suppressing insurrection would encourage 'the gentry to remain in their houses during the winter'.[77] The magistrates of the area it was claimed had done all they could 'for the public good' but were not helped by indiscipline in the ranks of the yeomanry such as the Kerry Militia and the Scots Regiment who were accused of rioting with each other in late August.[78]

Expressing fear of a civil war breaking out in May 1797, John Pomeroy, son of Lord Harberton, believed that the family stood to lose its extensive property at Carbury, which bordered with the Downshire estate, as there was now a 'rebellious disposition among the lower classes of people'.[79] After the death of Hatch in September, Lord Downshire must have worried that the same fate might befall his own estate at Edenderry, which was now without an agent. In December he visited the town for the first time since 1789, where he found things to be in a distressed state, and immediately wrote to Cooke requesting more troops to be sent there.[80]

The seizure by Defenders of a boat destined for Philipstown with a consignment of arms had, according to Downshire, 'made a deep impression on the minds of the disaffected here', who were growing in confidence all the time.[81] The yeomanry and some of the 'well affected' had fled into the town of Edenderry as a result for refuge. The marquis appealing to Cooke to act on the matter was writing 'to save the country'.[82] In a letter to the editor of the *Press* newspaper from a person at Edenderry using the pseudonym 'Humanus', the continued loyalty on the part of the Protestant community at Edenderry was stated. The writer maintained that they were 'all loyal persons' anxious to root out the Defender conspiracy at Edenderry.[83] The troops acquired by the marquis garrisoned the town of Edenderry. In 1798 the Defenders and United Irishmen would not have the same freedom of movement to carry out their outrages.

4. The 1798 rebellion: Edenderry's part

In his article 'The 1798 rebellion in north Leinster', Liam Chambers states that many historians rarely write about why rebellion did not happen.[1] King's County and in particular the Downshire estate at Edenderry had been heavily disturbed during the 1790s and it was reasonable to assume that the area would pose a problem for the government should rebellion break out. However, this was not the case and, as Jeanne Winder's comments, 'when the political situation reached boiling point in 1798, the dry land in King's County seems to have been saturated with military presence as the bogs were with water'.[2] The garrisoning of the town, the exertions of the magistrates and military ensured that no rebellion would break out on the estate in 1798. The government forces employed on the Downshire estate had managed to pacify much of King's County, helped by the issuing of an insurrection act in April 1798, and an order from General Abercromby on 14 March that King's County was to be disarmed.[3] This was followed by the posting of a proclamation in King's County in April by Abercromby threatening of the dire consequences the people would face if they failed to hand in their weapons.[4] The stationing of troops at Edenderry who lived at free quarters among suspected rebels had a major effect in quietening the area.[5] The local commander of government troops in King's County, General Dunne, was particularly successful in collecting firearms, indeed even loyalists were requested to have their arms registered.[6] On 1 April, Dunne had taken possession of over 1,000 muskets and countless other weapons, although a lack of pikes handed in showed that some were intent on the rebellion going ahead.[7]

General Dunne had also succeeded in having several Defenders and United Irishmen prosecuted at the spring assizes of 1798, possibly helped by the brother of Patrick and James Stubs who helped convict 'a notorious Defender and robber' at the assizes.[8] This was in contrast to the 1797 assizes when only one Defender, Farrell Cuffe, had been sentenced.[9] The returns of United Irishmen for 1798 stated that some 6,500 were active in King's County in April.[10] The arrest of the United Irish leaders at Oliver Bond's house in Dublin on 12 March provided the government with evidence that a rebellion was planned and ready to commence.

The delegate of the United Irishmen for King's County who was sent to the meeting of the societies executive, said to be a man named Flanagan from Tullamore, escaped arrest at Bond's house but turned approver. He in

turn relayed vital information to General Dunne and the leaders of the
various baronies were apprehended and the plans were counteracted and
foiled. Without this information from Flanagan, General Dunne commented
that King's County would have been 'as bad as Kildare'.[11] That the United
Irishmen were still active in King's County is ascertained in a letter in late
May which claimed that a John McMahon had left Dublin to 'call at the
camps for the King's County'.[12]

The events that enfolded in Co. Kildare prevented the rebels at the
Downshire estate from mobilizing as the military presence at Edenderry
increased after 24 May when the rebellion in Kildare began. The Defenders
and United Irishmen from the Downshire estate would see action in 1798
when they joined with the Kildare rebels at Rathangan, Clonard and
Timahoe. The terrain around the estate, mainly made up of bog, allowed the
rebels to attack and withdraw back into the bogs, which was put to great
effect at the battle of Rathangan.

Writing in his memoirs of the rebellion, Musgrave highlights the plight
of the inhabitants of the village of Rathangan some ten Irish miles from
Edenderry. The attack on Rathangan on 26 May 1798 by several thousand
rebels and the subsequent murder of 19 Protestants was comparable in
Musgrave's eyes with the well-documented slaughter of Protestants at
Scullabogue where nearly 100 people were massacred. As the rebellion
began in Co. Kildare, buoyed by early successes such as at Prosperous, rebels
from the heavily garrisoned Downshire estate organized to fight beyond the
county boundary.

From 24 May 1798 rebels had begun to mass on the outskirts of the
village of Rathangan, aided by the vastness of the bog, and the smoke of the
smouldering houses in the surrounding countryside which was proof to the
inhabitants of Rathangan of an impending attack.[13] The wife of the local
yeomanry captain and agent for the duke of Leinster, James Spenser, unaware
of the rebel's intentions, wrote to Viscount Harberton stating that, 'a number
of people had run away' and that the taking up of arms and pikes was
increasing all the time.[14] However the rebels were said to have numbered
close to 5,000 and a party of these were led by 'Captain' Casey from
Edenderry, whose brother had been apprehended for his part in the failed
attack on the Charter school in 1797.[15] Although no pitched battle was
fought at the Downshire estate during the rebellion, the battle of Rathangan
featured a large body of rebels from Edenderry fighting against the
Edenderry yeomanry who had come to aid the loyalists at Rathangan.

The South Cork Militia had withdrawn from Rathangan under Captain
Langton on 25 May, but James Spenser disobeyed orders to go to Sallins and
so was left to defend Rathangan with his local yeomanry force.[16] The rebels
attacked at three o'clock on 26 May accompanied with 'dreadful yells and
shouts' and immediately attacked the home of Spenser, who according to

Musgrave was an obnoxious figure to the rebels.[17] However, as agent for the duke of Leinster, Spenser would have been perceived by some of the rebels to have been 'friendly'. Despite this, he and four yeomen were piked and 'mangled' to death, while two other yeomen took up arms with the rebels.[18] Some years later Richard Musgrave recalled the sectarian nature of the rebels who murdered one man because he could not make the sign of the cross and who rejoiced in killing others declaring, 'there goes another Protestant'.[19] While it is clear that Musgrave wrote his memoirs with considerable bias, the atrocities carried out at Rathangan were some of the worst witnessed in the entire rebellion.

The rebels now controlled Rathangan but the arrival of government reinforcements was imminent and the threat of a similar attack on Edenderry prompted worried officers writing to Castlereagh from Edenderry to say that 'without reinforcements this country and a number of his majesties loyal subjects will inevitably be destroyed'.[20] Lt-Col. Mahon was dispatched from Tullamore and was accompanied by the Edenderry yeomanry to Rathangan, where they made little advance as they were heavily fired upon from every window of the village, incurring heavy losses believed to be as many as 26.[21] On 28 May the North Cork Militia and Lt-Col. Longfield recaptured the village and the rebels began to 'fly in every direction'.[22] The troops were said to be 'in want of everything' as the rebels had 'destroyed everything in and near the town'.[23]

According to Lt-Col. Dunne, the rebels who had been in possession of Rathangan intended to 'overrun the part of King's County adjoining Kildare, and to advance to Edenderry'.[24] The situation appeared to be desperate and Dunne exclaimed that the yeomanry forces were not of much use in fighting the rebels. The protection of the entire King's County was now left to 200 of the South Cork Militia and they had 'neither infantry or cannon'.[25] Many of the rebels were now camped at the bog at Timahoe under the command of William Aylmer. The contingent from Edenderry led by Captain Casey marched towards Carbury, where they re-visited the home of Stephen Sparks.

In the aftermath of the attack on the Charter school in Carbury in 1797, the Wicklow Militia remained posted at the home of Sparks, who believed that Defender activity placed him and his family in 'imminent and extreme danger'.[26] In September 1797 Sparks had received an anonymous letter telling him that if he regarded his life and that of his family he would leave the area at once. He was given until 1 October to leave by which time the writer assured Sparks that he would 'assist my true friends to the interests of Ireland' in murdering him.[27] Fleeing from defeat at Rathangan, Casey led a party of rebels believed to have been 2,000 strong in attacking the Charter school on 30 May 1798. This was to avenge the failed attack a year previously and to deny the use of the building to the military, which contained arms belonging to the Canal Company. Casey was well aware that the Wicklow Militia had vacated the school six days earlier, and the house was set fire to, forcing Sparks and the pupils to abandon the school.[28]

The rebels from Edenderry under Casey's command now enjoyed the freedom to manoeuvre, something they had been unable to do since the garrisoning of the town the previous winter. The rebels having seen the effectiveness of Lt-Col. Longfield move his troops via the canal 'let off the water of two or three levels of land' after he had passed through Edenderry.[29] On 5 June 1798 General Champagne went to Edenderry for troops to help disperse Aylmer's camp at Timahoe. Accompanying him were the canal yeomanry led by Adam Williams (who was married to Cartland's daughter) and the Edenderry yeomanry under John Wakely. The party advanced from Edenderry and cleared the camp located on an island on 8 June.[30] A large number of prisoners were taken back to Edenderry, where a prison had been improvised and to which the victors brought with them 'a considerable booty'.[31] The 'firmness and discipline' of Gough and Williams ensured that the rebel camp was completely destroyed.[32]

The government forces pursued the rebellion in Kildare with firmness and on 20 June 'crushed' a party of rebels at Edenderry.[33] The marquis of Downshire wrote to Cooke quite alarmed that 'the yeomanry and some well affected people who have fled there have as yet been able to contain themselves in my town of Edenderry'.[34] Downshire was hoping that Cooke would not neglect the situation, as Edenderry was, he claimed, 'a strong post and commands a great share of the country' and was for this reason 'worthy of attention'. He added that he had received numerous letters from the magistrates at Edenderry looking for support and in particular ammunition.

The battle of Foxes Hill, six Irish miles from Edenderry, on 30 June was a 'little known but intense clash',[35] which again involved rebels and yeomanry from Edenderry. The major of the Limerick City Militia, John Ormsby, received word that 'a large body of rebels has assembled on a hill six Irish miles from this town' and immediately proceeded to disperse them.[36] The Edenderry yeomanry under Captain Wakely were sent to cut off the rebel's retreat and when Ormsby arrived he found some three hundred men ready to give battle.

The rebels fled into the bog where the yeomanry had them 'cut to pieces in every direction out of the bog'.[37] The number that were killed, Ormsby estimated at 100, which was a terrible loss for the rebels. Among the casualties was 'Captain' Casey who had managed to kill two of the militia horses. Casey along with his brother was brought back to Edenderry as he belonged to that town and was hanged 'where he now remains', as Ormsby reported the next day.[38] The capture of 'Captain' Casey was a major bonus for the yeomanry as he had been a heroic figure in rebel eyes. When he was captured it was discovered he was wearing the overcoat of James Spenser, the murdered yeoman from Rathangan, and he also had boots belonging to Semple, another yeoman killed in that attack.[39] This is would seem definitely sealed his fate. The defeat of the rebels at Foxes Hill claimed Ormsby was due mainly to the exertions of the Limerick City Militia who he claimed would 'have burned down every house, and killed every man they met had I not restrained them'. His militia he believed were the 'most desperate fellows on earth and I am sure loyal; not a man received the slightest wound'.[40] Ormsby also expressed gratitude to George Brown from Edenderry who had volunteered and was 'forward on all occasions' and who on seeing a rebel officer took from him a large green standard which was brought back to Edenderry.[41] The standard known as the 'Whitechurch' flag can be seen today in Ballindoolin House, four miles from Edenderry.

The success of the Edenderry yeomanry at Foxes Hill had helped divert the threat of rebellion reaching the Downshire estate, and many rebels captured at Foxes Hill were brought back to Edenderry for court martial.[42] Their trials must have been postponed owing to the threat that still existed in the area, as William Hartigan mentions in a letter to Downshire that he was disillusioned to hear that the trials of these 'traitors' were cancelled and that he despaired 'of ever seeing them hanged'.[43] On 7 July the Limerick City Militia and Captain Wakely's yeomanry attacked and dispersed rebels camped on Viscount Harberton's demesne near Timahoe.[44]

Prior to the rebellion, the Revd Mogue or Moses Kearns, a priest of the diocese of Ferns, had served in the parish of Ballyna in Co. Kildare, close to the village of Clonard. As the Wexford rebels moved into the midlands, Kearns believed that a sufficient cache of arms could be secured at Clonard.[45] The home of Lt-Col. Tyrell, which was defended by 27 men, was the target for the rebels who now consisted of men from Wicklow, Wexford, Kildare and also included Edenderry rebels that had survived the battles of Rathangan and Foxes Hill. The rebels had begun to gather at Timahoe on 10 July, the garrison at Edenderry it seems being unaware of their location.[46] The garrison at Edenderry consisted of over 200 men, and as such not likely to be threatened by the rebels.

The rebel attack began on 11 July when Tyrell's defence of just 27 men was put to the test against an estimated 3,000 rebels. The Kinnegad and Edenderry yeomanry aided by the Northumberland Fencibles under Col Blake dispersed the rebels who could not withstand the 'dreadful fire of grape and round shot',[47] and the rebel dead was estimated at over 65.[48] Over 1,300 ball cartridges were fire at the rebels who dispersed and made their way to the Carbury Hill where they camped on the night of 11 July.

According to Joseph Holt, the Wicklow rebel, in his memoirs, 'harsh words were spoke' among the rebels on Carbury Hill in the wake of defeat at Clonard.[49] The rebels continued their plunder wreaking havoc on the homes of Richard Grattan Esq., Mr O'Farrell and Mr Nagle.[50] Rebels who were 'onwards of a thousand at camp at Carbury' also plundered the home of Viscount Harberton of its possessions.[51] The rebels claimed to the viscount's clerk, Brian Ford, to have been from Wicklow and Wexford, but almost certainly included men from Edenderry, familiar with the area.

The military at Edenderry were preparing themselves for an imminent attack on the town by the rebels who were 'in great force at Carbury hill'.[52] Col. Gough of the Limerick City Militia immediately left Edenderry, accompanied by 200 Dragoon guards and ten of Captain Wakely's troop to engage the rebels and found that their march was 'easily traced as they had left the country in flames where they had passed'. Having passed through Johnstown, which Gough found 'entirely consumed', and having been 'witness to their horrid conduct'; he prepared to give them battle at Knockderig Hill, some 15 kilometres from Edenderry.[53] The rebels were dispersed across the bog and countryside and more than 150 were killed by the militia and yeomanry. Once again, the spirit and 'gallant manner of the officers and soldiers' was crucial in the defeat of the rebels who were relieved of '16 fat bullocks, 53 horses and 7,000 yards of new linen'.[54]

The final encounter of the rebels from Edenderry came with the defeat at the battle of Knightstown Bog where, fleeing with the Wicklow and Wexford rebels, they had hoped to link up with their counterparts in Louth and Meath. Retreating from this setback, Col. Anthony Perry and the Revd Mogue Kearns, leaders of the Wexford contingent, were captured at Clonbullogue in King's County by two yeomanry officers, John Ridgeway and Samuel Robinson. They were taken to Edenderry and having been sentenced by court martial on 21 July they were hanged on Blundell Hill, overlooking the town. At their court martial in Edenderry it was claimed that Perry had been extremely communicative with the magistrates and 'gratified the enquiries of every person who spoke to him, and made such a favourable impression that many regretted his fate'.[55] At the moment of execution it was claimed that Kearns had voiced his anger at Perry for the information he had told his captors. He had also on given information under the threat of pitch capping at Gorey on 23 May.[56] The rebellion which had threatened the Downshire estate since late May was finally crushed.

However, according to Paddy Heaney, a local historian, 1,000 rebels gathered near Tullamore ready to march to Wexford under the command of James Morris in August. They were dispersed by a Revd O'Meara, a Roman Catholic priest from Tullamore, and when returning towards Edenderry the local yeomanry routed them.[57] The final episode of the 1798 rebellion at the Downshire estate occurred in September when the defeated French troops were transported through Edenderry along the Grand Canal on their way to Dublin.[58] Along the route, people gathered to see the captured French soldiers who with 'nonchalance and merriment' sang the *Marseillaise*.[59]

6 Celtic cross erected in 1874 over the grave of the
Revd Mogue Kearns and Col. Anthony Perry
hanged on Blundell Hill, 21 July 1798

The murder of Mary and Esther Grattan, at the estate of Viscount
Harberton at Carbury, showed how deep rooted was the sectarian nature of
the United Irishmen and Defenders. On the same night as the rebels
retreating from Clonard were camped at Carbury Hill and looted Newbury
Hall, the Grattan sisters were murdered by four men from Edenderry. They
were the only Protestants working for the viscount and were unhappy with
the rebels plundering the house. The accused men, Andrew Kenny, Thomas
McCan, John Bermingham and Henry Kilmurray, were involved in an
argument with the sisters and attested that they would 'put them out of their
way'.[60] The women were murdered and their bodies dumped in a pond at
the estate.

At the trial of the accused, Brian Ford, clerk for Viscount Harberton, gave
evidence that he saw the men take the women away and that he had heard
screams.[61] Another witness, Robert Noon, stated that the women's clothes

were intact when they were recovered; dispelling rumours that they had been raped. Prior to the rebellion it seems that the men had feloniously cut timber belonging to the estate, for which they were duly whipped. Despite transportation files existing for the men at the National Archives,[62] other evidence suggests that they were hanged at the place where they had committed the murder.[63]

The Quaker community at Edenderry also endured many of the hardships of the rebellion of 1798. In January, 'Friends' visited the home of Francis Metcalf but did not succeed in convincing him that by maintaining an armed guard at his house he made himself a target for the Defenders. The minutes of the monthly meetings of the Quakers at Edenderry show that, although they were a peaceful community who detested violence, some of their members could not resist securing weapons to defend themselves from attack. At the February meeting it was revealed that Francis Milner had not destroyed his gun, and he and Metcalf were both 'disunited' from the Society.[64]

Others such as Walter Chunl in March and Samuel Neale in June had their guns destroyed. The fear and panic experienced by the Quakers at Edenderry can be seen in the actions of Alexander Forbes Forrester, who along with a group of men broke into a house and took up arms to defend themselves with, for which he was also 'disunited'. Unlike their Protestant neighbours, most Quakers remained in their homes during the rebellion, and some like William Pim gave the rebels food and was left unharmed. Others such as John Gatchell were not so lucky, and after been accused of spying for the local magistrates he was shot dead.[65]

Although the Downshire estate had been spared the general horrors of the rebellion when compared with other areas of the country, there still existed a simmering discontent in the aftermath of the rebellion. In September Pilkington Homan wrote to the marquis of Downshire thanking him for the use of his house at Edenderry during the rebellion, and stating that he wished to remain there until the winter has passed. The invasion of the French had 'influenced the minds of the rebellious people', and his family's safety would be secured in the garrisoned town.[66] A shortage of provisions and employment was not helped by the large numbers of people who had fled from the villages of Clonbullogue and Rathangan to the estate. The 'hardships and danger'[67] that the people endured had not been averted and Brownrigg was writing in December asking that the barrack at Edenderry be filled with its full complement of 100 men.[68] A detachment of four officers, two sergeants, one drum and 50 rank and file soldiers were sent to Edenderry in late 1798.[69] Further damage to the canal by rebels still intent of subverting the law was reported and William Evans, barrack master of the Grand Canal, believed that it was 'indispensably necessary to guard the land from future damage' and asked for a small body of men to keep watch on the canal line at Edenderry, so that trade could be maintained with the capital.[70]

The arrears and failure of the tenants to pay rent to the marquis did not improve during 1798, and for about six months after the death of Hatch, Francis Synge endeavoured to clear Hatch's debt of £20,000.[71] Synge put pressure on tenants to pay what they owed; however he was not interested in taking on the job on a full-time basis.[72] Some of the tenants who could not pay the rent wrote to Downshire for leniency. One was James Moorhead, a school teacher, who included references from the Revd Lambart and Thomas Grattan, MD.[73] In March 1798, James Mooney was also looking for Downshire's help to stop Synge proceeding with a case against him.[74] The estate was out of lease and had not been properly surveyed in several years, and the numerous shopkeepers and merchants were all suffering from the effect of the economic decline and rebellion. These included Joshua Eves, a butcher, Mr Root, a tobacconist, and Arthur Keating, 'a poor old gunsmith'. During the rebellion Synge had attempted to conclude his affairs at Edenderry but 'was uncertain who will survive the present rebellion' and so set down an account of the arrears 'should anything befall me during these times'.[75] However, Synge noted that because of the outbreak of rebellion there was 'no prospect of any rents being paid for some time to come, at least not about Edenderry'.[76]

The marquis did not pay much attention to the estate at Edenderry during 1798; his estate house at Blessington was damaged by rebels to the cost of £10,000[77] and the area said to have been in a 'shocking state'.[78] Rebellion in counties Down and Antrim had threatened the family residence at Hillsborough, but by July 1798 however, the area was reported to have been restored to quiet.[79] Moves to bring about improvements at the estate after the rebellion seemed to have fallen on deaf ears, and no agent was put in place until October when John Brownrigg accepted the position.[80] In October, John Robinson proposed to establish a branch of the linen trade at Edenderry to be run by the family of his late sister's husband, Thomas Jackson. The value of the estate, Robinson believed, could be increased by manufacturing and that it was the 'only way to restore the town of Edenderry again to a state of recovery from its present ruinous situation'.[81]

In the aftermath of the rebellion there were many claims made to the government for losses incurred during the rebellion. These included loss of goods, livestock and damage to property and these were numerous at the Downshire estate. The motives of the rebels can be questioned when one takes into account the items stolen from people, as it seems that some were just intent on providing for their families and took advantage of the public disorder to do so. The Palmers of Rahan, Charles and Amos, both members of the local yeomanry reported sheep stolen from them.[82]

The attack on the home of Viscount Harberton by the rebels camped on Carbury Hill on 12 July showed how eager the rebels were to carry off whatever goods they could. The viscount was awarded over £3,000 in compensation for the loss of furniture, wine, horses and linen. Although Edenderry was heavily garrisoned the rebels still managed to steal some forty sheep that were in the possession of Henry Odlum as he passed through the town. The village of Clonbullogue suffered greatly in the rebellion, and rebels from the Downshire estate made off from the homes of James Moody, Henry Hickey and Michael Poole with furniture, potatoes and clothes. The homes of yeomen were not exempt from plunder, as James Mooney discovered, the rebels taking bacon and sheep amongst other items. The damage that the rebels had caused to the Grand Canal amounted to over £7,000.[83]

5. Aftermath: courts martial and poverty

Recalling a visit to Edenderry in 1817, John Gough highlighted how the rebellion of 1798 had 'reduced Edenderry from a good town to a poor village'.[1] The decline of the town, according to Gough, was also influenced by the 'mismanagement of mercenary agents and absentee landlords' and that the town was being rebuilt in a neat manner with only a few 'of the old ruinous buildings preserving'.[2] The town in Gough's opinion had progressed when it fell into the hands of the Hill family in 1786, and because of the marquis' untimely death it had failed to recover. The comments of Charles Coote further outline the decline of the estate when he described the 'miserable and shabby appearance' of the town with 'many houses falling to ruin' and predicted that the town would soon 'be a heap of ruins'.[3]

The rebellion had been quashed at the Downshire estate and many of the rebels brought to trial, imprisoned and listed for transportation. The Edenderry yeomanry were still engaged in apprehending rebels and were writing of the 'necessity of a barrack and a respectable garrison'.[4] There were no provisions for extra troops to be stationed at Edenderry even though John Brownrigg, the new agent for Lord Downshire, maintained that the 'greatest villains, rebels and United Irishmen in the Kingdom' were living at the estate.[5] Numerous requests for more troops were made, and the possibility of extending the barracks was raised.[6] In December 1799, Brownrigg wrote to Captain Evans, barrack master of the canal, that 'no person living knows the necessity of a barrack and a respectable garrison in this post better than you' and that a detachment was needed in Glann 'between Fullards and the Quakers burial ground and some as far as Jack Darby's at Drumcooley'.[7] The Kerry Militia, who were stationed at Edenderry after the rebellion, had not taken up lodging at Mrs Jackson's house and the militia officer, Capt. Mullins was said to be living five miles from the town.[8]

The high sheriff and justices of the peace were alarmed to learn that convicted rebels were to be released, many fearing that new plots would be formed against the yeomanry and the magistrates who had been 'active in preserving the county from open rebellion'.[9] The breakdown in law and order continued despite the efforts of the yeomanry, who failed to prevent many robberies including those on the mail coaches carrying post to the capital.[10] Some success was achieved when the yeomanry apprehended Nicholas Kavanagh of Carrick, described as the 'greatest robber in that country', who had used the pretence of rebellion to plunder many homes on the Downshire estate.[11] An account of secret service money paid out to Shawe Cartland also indicates that both he and the yeomanry were still active after the rebellion in apprehending rebels and villains. Indeed, on 30 January 1800 he received £56 for 'the discoveries of mail robbers' in King's County.[12] Other such as Viscount Harberton's clerk, Brian Ford, was handsomely rewarded for information supplied to the government.

The trials and court martials that followed after the rebellion detail the activities of Defenders and United Irishmen at the Downshire estate. The trial of Sir Duke Giffard at Philipstown assizes on 19 August 1800 showed how deep rooted the conspiracy at Edenderry was. Giffard, a wealthy landowner whose lands bordered the Downshire estate, stood accused of conspiring to murder Charles Palmer, esq., a local magistrate and yeoman. The court heard how Giffard had paid Charles Glinn £20 and offered him the forge at Castlejordan, Co. Meath, if he would murder Palmer. In June, Brownrigg wrote to the marquis informing him of this case and asking him had he heard about 'our poor fool Lord Giffard who is lodged in Kilmainham' and for whom no bail had been taken 'although large sums were offered'.[13] However, like many of the accused both before and after the rebellion, several good character statements were given and Giffard was acquitted.[14]

Similarly James Doneghan was found not guilty at the assizes of being in the 'command of a body of men' that styled themselves Defenders at the end of 1799 and that he also endeavoured to cut down timber to make pike handles.[15] Giving evidence on behalf of the government, Patrick De Bor, told the court that Doneghan had approached him and others at Monasteroris chapel and told them to have their arms ready, that the day of 'long threatening will come at last'. This, according to De Bor, was proof that the Defenders were still active at the Downshire estate in 1799 and awaiting another arrival of the French. In his evidence De Bor also claimed that Doneghan had asked him to cut timber for him at Mr Beaumans for 'we that are in Edenderry are so watched by the guard that we cannot get out'. Showing that a sense of fear existed in the aftermath of rebellion, De Bor insisted that he had told the defendant that they 'would not venture their lives for anybody else'. However, the Revd William Lambart and George Matthews, a yeoman, testified that Doneghan had been 'honest and industrious' during the rebellion thus securing his release.[16] The trial of James Carroll also reached the same conclusion after Shawe Cartland gave witness for the convict who was accused of a murder during the rebellion.[17] Prior to the rebellion both Carroll and his father had been employed on Cartland's land at Lumville. The informer, Patrick De Bor of Ballindoolin, was also implicated in rebellion during the trial of Edward Allen and Michael Costello, who claimed that they had tried De Bor and William Welsh at a Defender court in 1796 on the charge that they had struck Frank Gore. The defendants, who were tried for plotting to murder John Wakely of

Ballyburley, told the court that De Bor had been an active Defender in 1796 and had told them at his trial in Kennedy's bog that he did care for any of them and was prepared to meet his fate. Both De Bor and Welsh were released on the night of their trial in 1796, as the Defender, Captain Jellico, had not sanctioned such a gathering. The prisoners, Costello and Allen, were found guilty of conspiring to murder De Bor, Welsh and later Wakely but were released on security of their good behaviour.[18]

However, the trial of the Hayes brothers, William and James, did not have the same outcome after the court had heard how they had planned to murder Samuel Robinson, esq., Andrew Higgins and Thomas Smith. Their crime was that they had been involved in the capture of the Wexford rebels, Kearns and Perry, who were hanged at Edenderry in July 1798. If they could murder Robinson, claimed William Hayes, they might 'do what they pleased in this country'.[19] The court was also told by William Carron that it had been William Hayes and John Crowley's job to meet Robinson on the road and to murder him. According to the witness, Hayes was heard to say that his gun would make 'a riddle of Robinson's carcase'. The prisoners were found guilty and were transported for seven years on board the *Anne* to New South Wales in 1800.[20]

The residents of Philipstown wrote to Dublin Castle in June 1800 requesting courts martial for the 'several depredations', which were being committed in the baronies adjoining them by a 'desperate gang of villains who had infested it'.[21] Subscriptions had been offered to entice people to come forward with information regarding these 'atrocious acts'.[22] The Quakers were also conducting their own investigation into the rebellion and found in February 1799 that Thomas Neale did not take up arms but had only entered the army for his own protection, as the Defenders had threatened his life. Accordingly the meeting of Quakers found him not guilty and he was 'reunited' into the community.[23]

The decline of the fortunes of the estate continued after the rebellion with the roads and bridges in bad repair, 'the idle effects of the rebellion still obvious', as Charles Coote recorded three years later.[24] Provisions of most kinds were scarce, the peasantry surviving on a diet of potatoes and oatmeal.[25] The conditions of the poor were not helped by the arrival of beggars and Connaught cottiers at the estate, which forced Brownrigg to employ heavy-handed tactics to remove them from the town.[26] The issue of providing relief and provisions for the poor on the estate caused a disagreement between agent and landlord in July 1800 when Brownrigg was forced to remind the marquis of his responsibilities 'that the gentlemen of the area were becoming perturbed by the lack of his subscription'.[27] The marquis responded by asking Brownrigg whether he was doing everything that was 'right and becoming' on his behalf.[28] Numerous attempts to relieve the plight of the poor had been adopted at Edenderry including the distribution of a consignment of peas and onions that Downshire sent which he hoped would 'prove useful to the poor soup eaters of Edenderry'.[29] In June 1800 Brownrigg began giving relief to some 30 families 'gratis' which he believed was necessary 'for all the aged and the infirm would perish if not furnished with meal at reduced prices'.

The extension of the Grand Canal to the town was delayed owing to the damage caused by rebels who had cut breaches in the bank of the canal. The marquis gave £1,000 in 1799 for the branch to be constructed to the town in order to revive the fortunes of the estate.[30] Providing work for the poor during times of distress was the measure proposed by James Brownrigg, who replaced his father as agent towards the end of 1800, seeing it as a means of discouraging the dishonest elements of society.[31] The new agent at Edenderry was hoping for an improvement of fortunes there and wrote to the marquis informing him that the engineer and the pickaxes were busy cutting the branch of the canal,[32] as were the men employed clearing the town of the 'rubbish and ruin' in preparation for the building of a thosel.[33] The building of the thosel or market house was not feasible at this time as Downshire feared 'that the price of materials have not fallen sufficiently for having laid any stone for the rapid erection of the plans'.[34] Similarly the marquis again rejected proposals for some industry to be promoted at Edenderry, as the Quakers were people 'who make promises to themselves' and that the products of a tan yard were 'an offensive thing in a town'.[35] A survey of 1806 carried out by the Busby brothers found that Edenderry was 'well fit as a seat for manufacture' owing to the abundance of water, peat, cheap labour and the possibility of mining lead in and near the town.[36]

The marquis was preoccupied with his opposition to the Act of Union throughout the years 1799–1800 and eventually lost most of his privileges when the Irish parliament was abolished. In January 1800 he wrote to Brownrigg asking 'a little after poor Edenderry' and 'how are things a going on there', suggesting that the estate was the least of his worries at this time.[37] More importantly he enquired as to the 'sentiments of the gentry' of Edenderry regarding 'this dammed union'. Downshire wished to know if he could count on the votes of Cartland, Wakely and Tyrell should a meeting of the county be called to vote on the matter.[38] The Act of Union was a major event of the day and was debated at Edenderry, where pamphlets were found posted on the road to Philipstown. This particular debate between Darby Tracy and Denis Feagan, a breeches maker at Edenderry had a number of editions such was its popularity.[39] The dangers of writing letters were also outlined to Brownrigg who was told that the marquis could not direct post to him at Edenderry in 'his usual hand or sealed with his coat of arms'.[40]

The estate was still out of lease during this period, some tenants it was claimed had not paid any rents for nine years and Brownrigg was reluctant to evict tenants, such was 'the miserable state of the lower class of people'.[41]

Several gentlemen in the town, including Pilkington Homan were to be served with ejectments but were so numerous and all suffering from the lack of provisions that Brownrigg ' thought it a great piece of cruelty to add legal persecution to their suffering'.[42] However, heavy-handed tactics were adopted on various occasions by Brownrigg, who had taken possession of the mill for which 'Collins the miller cursed' him on his knees.[43] Several other buildings and cabins had their roofs pulled down by the soldiers to prevent re-entry which Brownrigg hoped would create a sensation at the estate and force a payment from 'those who never intended paying it'.[44] These included Richard Martin with holdings in Ardenderry, Philip Hyland and James Connor. Opposing the bill for the Union, Cartland was assured by Downshire that he would not be harassed to pay any more arrears (which amounted to £1,300);[45] but when the bill passed into law, Downshire's attitude changed and he found that Cartland would have no excuse to pay his arrears. Likewise the other tenants in arrears, whom he referred to as 'Hatch's potwallopers', should also 'be well milked before they remove the crops from the ground'.[46]

The marquis died on 7 September 1801, aged 48, the strain of losing his government position and privy council membership being blamed for the decline in his health. The estate at Edenderry entered the 19th century continuing to dwindle into decline and unrest, much as it had done throughout the 1790s. The town was said to have one distillery and three windmills, but the barracks were considered a miserable lodging for the soldiers. Still discontented, the peasantry were so 'audacious and wicked that they plundered the honest industrious inhabitants of everything'. According to Brownrigg, not a night would pass when there was not an act of plunder where the peasants 'steal corn, dig the potatoes, milk the cows, carry off the hay and turf, which they carry off in open day by open force'.[47]

6. Conclusion: myth, legend and commemoration

The 1798 rebellion and the events of that period are still celebrated. As Tom Dunne aptly comments, '1798 has never passed into history because it never passed out of politics'.[1] At various stages when people have commemorated 1798 at Edenderry the politics of the day have over-shadowed proceedings. The bicentenary celebrations of the rebellion were linked to the Peace Process of Northern Ireland, which had been recently signed. Speaking at Monasteroris graveyard where the Wexford rebels, Kearns and Perry are buried, Thomas O'Connell told the gathering that the greatest tribute the people of today could pay to the memory of Kearns and Perry was to 'respect all differences of opinion and the right of others to express opinions, because that is the road to peace'.[2] The hope that the next generation of people at Edenderry would keep alive the memory of Kearns and Perry was also expressed by O'Connell, who believed that their grave would 'remain a place of pilgrimage in the future as it had been in the past'.[3]

Why is it that the 1798 rebellion is celebrated at Edenderry? The veneration, which the Wexford rebels have received, hanged by chance at Blundell Hill, has meant that much else of what occurred at the Downshire estate during the 1790s has been ignored and passed into oblivion. In 1898 and 1998 the commemorations made no mention of 'Captain' Casey, William Kennedy or Stephen Hyland. The role of Shawe Cartland and the Edenderry yeomanry were also overlooked, as were the innocent victims of the Defenders such as the Bagnalls or the Grattan sisters. The 1790s were a period of poverty, social distress and a period of anarchy when the Defenders played havoc on the local countryside. Commemorations at Edenderry have tended to ignore the plight of the ordinary person; instead Kearns and Perry, with a memorial stone at their execution spot and streets named in their honour, take the limelight.

The 1898 celebrations came during a period of Gaelic revival and a most impressive demonstration was held at Monasteroris graveyard to honour 'as true martyrs to the cause of liberty as ever breathed'.[4] A centenary commemorative committee was formed at Edenderry and people travelling from all across the midlands attended the celebrations. The gathering, assembled beneath the huge Celtic cross commissioned in 1874, were told

7 President Sean T. O'Kelly and Cardinal Gilroy at Edenderry in 1950.
The flag captured by George Brown at the battle of Foxes Hill in 1798,
and known as the 'Whitechurch' flag is hanging behind them.

that Kearns and Perry were 'strangled because they loved Ireland above any
other consideration', a comment greeted by huge applause.[5] A grand-
nephew of Mogue Kearns was invited to the commemoration, which called
on the people to 'advance the sacred cause of Ireland'.[6]

Similar scenes of commemoration were enacted on Carbury Hill in 1898,
where William Kennedy was hanged in 1797 for his part in the attack on the
Charter school. However, the crowd that gathered there did not commem-
orate Kennedy, but instead celebrated the date of the rebellion breaking out
in nearby Co. Kildare.[7] In July 1898 the Edenderry centenary committee
organized a demonstration on Carbury Hill said to have been attended by
3,500 people and a bonfire was lit on this occasion. No mention was made
in the 1898 or 1998 commemorations of Kennedy despite the existence of
many poems and songs referring to the brogue maker from Kishawanna.
Two of these songs include the lyrics, 'And home we then returned, Sparks'
house we burned, in recompense for Kennedy that died there on a tree' and
'it was on Carbury Hill our precious blood they spilled, when Kennedy our
hero, they hung him'.[8]

Although there was an enthusiastic commemoration of Kearns and Perry
at Edenderry in 1898, it must have been short lived, as the *King's County*

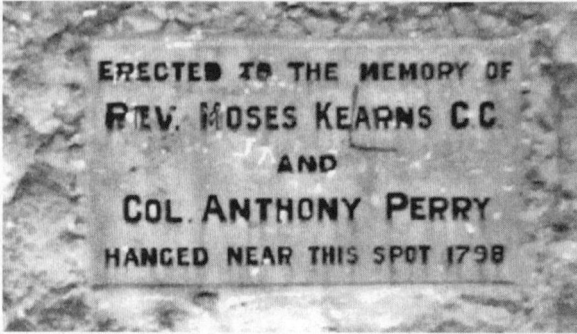

ERECTED TO THE MEMORY OF
REV. MOSES KEARNS C.C.
AND
COL. ANTHONY PERRY
HANGED NEAR THIS SPOT 1798

8. Memorial stone unveiled in 1986 by Sean MacBride
close to the spot where Kearns and Perry were
hanged on Blundell Hill in 1798

Chronicle reported ten years later, that the 'monument has fallen into neglect which threatens its complete ruin'. The Cumann Na Gaedhal movement had instituted a collection for the purpose of renovating the monument 'which marks the grave of two of Eire's bravest and devoted heroes'.[9] The memory of 1798 was again evoked in 1950 when President Sean T. O'Kelly visited Edenderry, where he was presented with a gun said to have been used by the rebels in 1798. The president spoke of Edenderry being 'a hallowed place' where the people had risen 'in defence of faith and fatherland'.[10] The 'Whitechurch' flag captured at the battle of Foxes Hill in 1798 by George Brown adorned the platform that the President spoke from. In June 1986, Sean Mac Bride unveiled the memorial to Kearns and Perry at Blundell Hill, where he also spoke of the sacrifices that the Wexford rebels had made.[11]

The myth and legend associated with the rebellion of 1798 at Edenderry has confused the memory of this period and much of what occurred has been replaced by stories of the hanging of Kearns and Perry. Many of these myths and legends are far- fetched, such as the claim that at the execution of the Wexford rebels, a 'shower of blood' rained down on the gathering. In like manner it was claimed that descendants of the executioners were born with rope marks on their necks.[12] Another of these stories told is that the bodies of Kearns and Perry were taken from Blundell Hill and their heads sewn back on by a Catherine O'Connell, who then had their bodies interred in Monasteroris graveyard.[13] However, this legend has been disputed down through the years by people such as Fr Joseph Hurley, who claimed in 1953 that he found the skull of Kearns at Cambridge University, said to have been taken there by the grandson of Captain Ridgeway who arrested the Wexford rebels in July 1798.[14] Another story is told how the relations of Kearns and Perry dug up the bodies in the middle of the night soon after their burial and brought them back to Wexford.[15] Another local figure of this period that has passed into oblivion and forgotten at local commemorations is Farrell Cuffe, the only Defender in the area convicted at the spring assizes in 1797. Cuffe was transported on board the *Minerva* to New South Wales in 1800, which included the Wicklow rebel Joseph Holt. In his personal account of the rebellion of 1798, Holt recalls the trip to New South Wales and describes Cuffe as a 'schoolmaster from King's County'.[16] During this trip Cuffe educated Holt's 12-year-old son and later set up a school in Sydney as well as owning a public house there. He was involved in the United Irish conspiracy in New South Wales in 1800 and was sentenced to receive 500 lashes for his part. In 1828 he was described as being married with one son and farming thirty acres.[17]

From the evidence discussed it is clear that the Downshire estate at Edenderry was affected by rebellion and disturbance during a period of economic decline, social and political unrest. That the Defenders wreaked havoc on the inhabitants of the estate is clear, as are the motives that lay behind their actions. The decline in the fortunes of the woollen industry and the subsequent poverty at Edenderry gave the Defenders a platform from which they emerged to take root and attack their Protestant neighbours.

The exertions of the minor gentry and dependants in apprehending Defenders and reporting to their landlord at Hillsborough and to Dublin Castle was justified, as they were seriously threatened by the Defenders. However, it also appears that personal debt, arrears and advancement were other reasons for this loyalty. The debt owed to the estate by Shawe Cartland was not cleared during the 1790s as he carried out his duties to maintain law and order at the estate. Similarly the Revd William Lambart's motives for his loyal exertions can be called into question, as it appears that personal advancement by way of the rectory of Monasteroris was his real goal.[18] The presence of the military at Edenderry in early 1798, along with the prosecution of Defenders at the assizes and the heavy-handed tactics of General Dunne, ensured that the rebellion did not break out at the Downshire estate in 1798.

This account of events of the 1790s at the Downshire estate in King's County, will I believe, help toward a greater understanding of the period by moving away from the myth and legend that is associated with 1798. The part played by Defenders such as 'Captain' Casey and William Kennedy deserve to be commemorated, as do the exertions of the Edenderry yeomanry, gentry and the innocent victims such as the Bagnalls. To understand this period we must be willing to accept that it was a time of poverty, distress and fear imposed by the Defenders, and not an heroic era as 1798 is often portrayed.

Appendix

Rental of the estate of the most noble Arthur Marquis of Downshire at Edenderry in the King's County due at Michaelmas and November 1797 (PRONI, Downshire papers D/607/R6/1B)

Ardbash
Shawe Cartland Esq.

Ardenderry
Thady Byrne
Widow Tracey
George Carmichael
Christopher Doran
Charles Dempsey
Pat Hynes
Pat Hickey
John Ward
James Whittaker
Robert Jackson
F Hynes
Sylvester Kelly
Edward Connor
Thomas Baily
Pat Collins (Miller)
John Darby
John Eason
Richard Grattan
James Heffernan
Philip Hyland
William Ridgeway
Laurence Shiels
William Glanan

Ballykillen
Shawe Cartland Esq.

Ballynanum
Shawe Cartland Esq.

Clonmullen
James Berry
Matthew McDermott
Widow Neale
Henry Brien
Joseph Barnes
Thomas Baily
Rev Henry Baily
William Burrows
Misses Bagnall
William Cartwright
Robert Fullard
Benjamin Williams

Clonmullen
Dr T Grattan (called Deerpark)
Robert Jackson
Michael Kelly
George Kelly (taken up in
    insurrection)
Rev William Lambart
Paul McDonagh
James Kennedy
George Telford
Late Francis Grattan
John Neale
William Tyrell
Robert Boylan
George Homan

Ellie North
Edward Kelly Jnr
James Hayes
Widow Dunn
Dan Woolaghan
Thomas Telford

Clonlack
John Brownrigg

Clonmeen
Dan Fitzpatrick
Hoey & Gordon
Widow Quinn
Widow Patk Dunn
William& James Seery
William& Patk Owens

Codd
Hugh&James Farrell
James Mooney
John&Ed Mooney
Rich&Hugh Mooney
Thos&Ed Roe

Coneyburrow & Derrycorris
Widow Anderson
Mr Atkinson
Edward Murray
Robert Coulton
Owen Murphy
John Hope
John&Dan Ryan
August Hurst
Widow Bryan
Dan Ford
William Byrne
John Coyne

Derryesker& Codd
Thomas Morrison
Wm&Marie Fitzsimons

Widow Nevin
Maura Fitzsimons

Cushaling (the threehold)
Bernard Tierney
David Homan
Nathaniel Taylor

Edenderry
Henry Arnot
James Berry
Murt McDermott
James Fry
William Barnes
Bryan Connor
James Connor
James Connor Jnr
Edward Connor
John Carroll
James Collins
John Corbally (gamekeeper)
Cavalry field (in meadow)
Hannah Curtis
Charles Doran
Michael Dunn
John Dennel
Widow Davie
Dan Dougherty
Joshua Eves
William Eves
William Egan
Robert Fullard (brewer)
John Gorman
Matt Gorman
Patrick Hickey
John Hickey
Michael Hyland
Lord Downshire's house
Thomas Hurst
William Jessop
William Killeen
John Kelly

Arthur Keating (gunsmith)
Charles Palmer
William Lynch
James McCann
William Lynch
Widow McMahon
James McEvoy
Richard Martin
James Moorhead
George Palmer
William Owens
John Ridgeway
Patrick Stanton
Mrs Tracey
Thomas Tinkler
James Usher
Edward Walsh
Patrick Walsh
Thomas Wheelan
William Warren
Laurence Ginn

Eskermore
George Fawcett
Thomas Fitzgerald

Rathmore
William Walsh
Shawe Cartland Esq.

Rathgreedan
Samuel Brennan

Big Shean
Pilkington Homan

Great Shean
George Clarke

Quaker Meeting House
Joshua Inman

Notes

ABBREVIATIONS

D/607	Downshire papers
D/617	
Harb. pap.	Harberton papers
IHS	*Irish Historical Studies*
NAI	National Archives of Ireland
NLI	National Library of Ireland
PRONI	Public Record Office of Northern Ireland
Reb. pap.	Rebellion papers

INTRODUCTION

1 Revd William Lambart to Thomas Pelham, 14 Oct. 1796 (NAI, Rebellion papers, 620/26/25).
2 Ruan O'Donnell, 'King's county in 1798', in William Nolan and Timothy P. O'Neill (eds), *Offaly history and society: interdisciplinary essays on the history of an Irish county* (Dublin 1998), pp 485–514.
3 Pádraig Mac Suibhne, *Kildare in 98* (Naas, 1978).
4 Liam Chambers, 'The 1798 rebellion in north Leinster', in Thomas Bartlett et al. (eds) *1798: a bicentenary perspective* (Dublin, 2003) p. 31.
5 Magistrates of King's County to Dublin Castle, 29 Jan. 1797 (NAI, Rebellion papers, 620/28/179).
6 Letter from Cecil S. Fitzpatrick, Archivist of the Grand Orange Lodge of Ireland to Mrs Pollard, Edenderry (Edenderry Public Library).
7 John Hatch to Lord Hillsborough, 27 Nov. 1786 (PRONI, Downshire papers, D/607/A/316).
8 John Hatch to Miss Blundell, 30 Jan. 1792 (PRONI, Downshire papers, D/607/A/455).

I. BACKGROUND TO EDENDERRY IN 1790

1 Philip Luckombe, *A tour through Ireland: wherein the present state of that kingdom is considered, and the most noted cities, towns, seats* (Dublin, 1780), p. 54.
2 A.P.W. Malcomson, 'The gentle Leviathan: Arthur Hill, 2nd marquis of Downshire, 1753–1801' in Peter Roebuck (ed.), *Plantation to partition: essays in Ulster history in honour of J.L. McCracken* (Belfast, 1981), p. 103.
3 Deirdre Lindsay, 'The rebellion papers: an introduction to the rebellion papers collection in the National Archives, Bishop Street, Dublin' in *Ulster Local Studies*, 18:2 (1997) pp 28–42.
4 Francis Synge to Lord Downshire, 7 Oct. 1797 (PRONI, D/607/A/539). Synge was a son-in-law of Hatch, and after his death tried to sort out his financial affairs.
5 Miss Blundell to John Hatch, 1 Sept. 1787 (PRONI, D/607/A/340).
6 John Hatch to Lord Bertie, 30 June 1781 (Berkshire Record Office, MIC 17/1/318, viewed at Edenderry Public Library).
7 Petition of Worsted Weavers in Edenderry to Lord Downshire, 5 Oct. 1810 (PRONI, D/607/C/234/12).

8 John Hatch to Lord Bertie, June 1779 (Berkshire Record Office, MIC 17/1/281).
9 Ibid.
10 Ibid.
11 John Hatch to Miss Blundell, 30 June 1783 (Berkshire Record Office, MIC 17/1/226).
12 Ibid.
13 John Hatch to Miss Blundell, 10 May 1784 (Berkshire Record Office, MIC 17/1/227).
14 John Hatch to Miss Blundell, 3 Aug. 1786 (Berkshire Record Office, MIC 17/1/243).
15 John Hatch to Miss Blundell, 10 May 1784 (Berkshire Record Office, MIC 17/1/227).
16 John Hatch to Lord Bertie, 30 June 1781 (Berkshire Record Office, MIC 17/1/318).
17 Ibid.
18 John Hatch to Miss Blundell, 10 May 1784 (Berkshire Record Office, MIC 17/1/227).
19 John Hatch to Lord Bertie, June 1779 (Berkshire Record Office, MIC 17/1/281).
20 John Hatch to Miss Blundell, 10 May 1779 (Berkshire Record Office, MIC 17/1/230).
21 Mairead Evans and Noel Whelan, *Edenderry through the ages* (Edenderry, 2000), p. 26.
22 John Hatch to Lord Sandys, 5 Aug. 1786 (PRONI, D/607/A/307).
23 John Hatch to Lord Sandys, 14 Dec. 1786 (PRONI, D/607/A/320).
24 Ibid.
25 John Hatch to Miss Blundell, 10 May 1779 (Berkshire Record Office, MIC 17/1/230).
26 Miss Blundell to John Hatch, 12 Mar. 1787 (PRONI, D/607/A/328).
27 John Hatch to Miss Blundell, 24 Aug. 1787 (PRONI, D/607/A/338).
28 John Hatch to Miss Blundell, 22 June 1787 (PRONI, D/607/A/333).
29 Miss Blundell to John Hatch, 1 Sept. 1787 (PRONI, D/607/A/340).
30 J.T. Gilbert (ed.), *Documents relating to Ireland, 1795–1804* (repr. Shannon, 1972), p. 39.
31 Charles W. Finney, *Records of Castro-Petre* (Kildare, 1978), p. 9.
32 *The Times*, 10 Oct. 1786.

2. SOCIAL UNREST, 1790–5

1 Pomeroy to Lord Harberton, 2 Aug. 1792 (PRONI, Harb. pap., T2954/4/24).
2 Miss Blundell to John Hatch, 15 Jan. 1793 (PRONI, D/607/A/454 A-B).
3 John Hatch to Miss Blundell, 5 Jan. 1793 (PRONI, D/607/A/453).
4 Thomas Bartlett, 'An end to the moral economy: The Irish militia disturbances of 1793' in *Past & Present*, 99 (1983), p. 49.
5 Sir Richard Musgrave, *Memoirs of the different rebellions in Ireland* (2nd ed., Dublin, 1801), p. 639.
6 Kildare County Assizes, 22 March 1792 (NLI, MS 9,208).
7 Ibid.
8 John Hatch to Lord Hillsborough, 10 April 1790 (PRONI, D/607/A/397).
9 John Hatch to Lord Hillsborough, 12 May 1791 (PRONI, D/607/A/417).
10 Charles W. Finney, *Records of Castro Petre* (Kildare, 1978), p. 16.
11 John Hatch to Lord Hillsborough, 18 Jan. 1791 (PRONI, D/607/A/411 A-B).
12 John Hatch to Miss Blundell, 10 April 1789 (PRONI, D/607/A/377).
13 Quoted in R.B. McDowell, *Irish public opinion, 1750–1800* (London, 1944), p. 32.
14 Inscription on Cartland Bridge, Ballycolgan, Edenderry.
15 *Dublin Evening Post*, 23 May 1796.
16 W.A. Maguire, 'Missing persons: Edenderry under the Blundell and the Downshires 1707–1922' in W. Nolan & T.P. O'Neill (eds), *Offaly: history and society* (Dublin, 1998), p. 545.
17 John Hatch to Lord Hillsborough, 18 Sept. 1792 (PRONI, D/607/A/449).
18 John Hatch to Miss Blundell, 30 Jan. 1793 (PRONI, D/607/A 455).
19 John Hatch to Miss Blundell, 7 Aug. 1794 (PRONI, D/607/A/472).

20 Miss Blundell to Hatch, 5 Jan. 1795 (PRONI, D/607/A /477 A-B).

21 Ruán O'Donnell, 'King's County in 1798' in Nolan & O'Neill (eds), *Offaly: history and society*, p. 487.

22 Lord Camden to Lord Downshire, 17 Aug. 1795 (PRONI, D/607/C/129).

23 Fenton Aylmer to Lord Downshire, 22 Nov. 1795 (PRONI, D/607/C/170).

24 Andrew Skinner and George Taylor, *Maps of the roads of Ireland* (Dublin, 1783), pp 83–5.

25 Henry S. Keating, *On the defence of Ireland; including observations on some other subjects connected therewith* (Dublin, 1795), p. 49.

26 Court Martial of Edward Allen and Michael Costello, 5 Feb. 1800 (NAI, Reb. Pap., 620/9/88).

3. DEFENDER DISTURBANCE AND 'STIRRINGS' OF THE FRENCH

1 Shawe Cartland to Thomas Pelham, 8 Aug. 1796 (NAI, Reb pap., 620/24/105).

2 Major Oliver Fairclough to Lord Downshire, 15 Oct. 1796 (PRONI, D/607/A/512).

3 Shawe Cartland to Thomas Pelham, 8 Aug. 1796 (NAI, Reb. pap., 620/24/105).

4 Ibid.

5 Ibid.

6 Ruth Delany, *The Grand Canal of Ireland* (Newton Abbot, 1973), p. 71.

7 Revd William Lambart to Lord Downshire, 14 Oct. 1796 (PRONI, D/607/A/511).

8 John Everard to Lord Downshire, 17 Oct. 1796 (PRONI, D/607/A/514).

9 Seamus O'Loinsigh, *The 1798 rebellion in Meath* (Dublin, 1997), p. 29.

10 William Lambart to Thomas Pelham, 14 Oct. 1796 (NAI, Reb. pap., 620/25/168).

11 Ibid.

12 Ibid.

13 Ibid.

14 Ibid.

15 Rev William Lambart to Edward Cooke, 25 Sept. 1796 (NAI, Reb., pap 620/25/117).

16 Revd William Lambart to Thomas Pelham, 6 Nov. 1796 (NAI, Reb. pap., 620/26/25).

17 Revd William Lambart to Lord Downshire, 24 Jan. 1797 (PRONI, D/607/A/526).

18 O'Loinsigh, *The 1798 rebellion in Meath*, p. 31.

19 John Hatch to Miss Blundell, 20 Feb. 1797 (PRONI, D/607/A/532).

20 John Hatch to Lord Downshire, 11 Jan. 1796 (PRONI, D/607/A/493).

21 Benjamin Glorney to Lord Downshire, 24 June 1796 (PRONI, D/607/A/502b).

22 John Hatch to Lord Downshire, 12 Jan. 1797 (PRONI, D/607/A/523).

23 Shawe Cartland to John Hatch, 28 Jan. 1797 (PRONI, D/607/A/528).

24 General Henry Eustace to Lord Downshire, 10 Feb. 1797 (PRONI, D/607/A/529).

25 Magistrates of the barony of Coolestown to Thomas Pelham, 31 Jan. 1797 (NAI, Reb. Pap. 620/28/179).

26 John Hatch to Lord Downshire, 17 Feb. 1797 (NAI, Reb. pap. 620/28/250).

27 *The Times*, 22 Sept. 1797.

28 John Wakely to Thomas Pelham, 26 April 1797 (NAI, Reb. pap. 620/29/319).

29 John Everard to Thomas Pelham, 26 April 1797 (NAI, Reb. Pap., 620/29/318).

30 O'Loinsigh, *The 1798 rebellion in Meath*, p. 33.

31 John Tyrell to Thomas Pelham, 30 June 1797 (NAI, Reb. pap. 620/28/170).

32 William Elliss to Thomas Pelham, 10 May 1797 (NAI, Reb. pap. 620/30/102).

33 Revd William Lambart to Thomas Pelham, 17 March 1797 (NAI, Reb. Pap. 620/29/184).

34 Revd William Lambart to Thomas Pelham, 16 April 1797 (NAI, Reb. pap. 620/29/268).

35 Ibid.

36 Ibid.
37 John Pomeroy to Viscount Harberton, May 1797 (PRONI, Harberton papers, T2954/8/13).
38 Letter from Alex Kerr, landowner near Carbury (NAI, Reb. pap. 620/30/36).
39 Revd William Lambart to Edward Cooke, 15 June 1797 (NAI, Reb. pap. 620/31/97).
40 Ibid.
41 Enclosed with letter from Shawe Cartland to Dublin Castle, 16 May 1797 (NAI, Reb. pap., 620/30/132).
42 MS at Edenderry Public Library (Local historical file).
43 Revd William Lambart to Edward Cooke, 10 May 1797 (NAI, Reb. pap., 620/30/47).
44 Kenneth Milne, *Irish charter schools, 1730–1830* (Dublin, 1997), p. 39.
45 Stephen Sparks to Thomas Pelham, 14 May 1797 (NAI, Reb. pap. 620/30/66).
46 Revd William Lambart to Edward Cooke, 10 May 1797 (NAI, Reb. pap., 620/30/47).
47 Ibid.
48 *The Press*, 16 Nov. 1797.
49 Liam Chambers, *Rebellion in Co. Kildare, 1790–1803* (Dublin 1998), p. 53.
50 *Dublin Evening Post*, 23 May 1797.
51 *The Press*, 16 Nov. 1797.
52 Chambers, *Rebellion in Co. Kildare*, p. 45
53 Examination of Stephen Hyland of New Chapel in the Co. Kildare (Blacksmith) (NAI, Reb. pap., 620/30/47).
54 *The Press*, 16 November 1797.
55 John Brownrigg to Edward Cooke, 27 Aug. 1797 (NAI, Reb. pap., 620/32/77).
56 Ibid.
57 *The Press,* 16 Nov. 1797.
58 *Freeman's Journal*, 19 May 1797.
59 Douglas Glynn, *Friends and 1798: Quaker witness to non-violence in 18th century Ireland* (Dublin, 1998), p. 34.
60 Ibid.
61 Shawe Cartland to Edward Cooke, 10 July 1797 (NAI, Reb. pap., 620/28/250).
62 Henry Stewart to Lord Downshire, 23 Sept. 1797 (PRONI, D/607/A/536).
63 John Hatch to Lord Downshire, rental lease of his lordship's lands at Edenderry, 1797 (PRONI, D/671/R6/1C).
64 Francis Synge to Lord Downshire, 7 Oct. 1797 (PRONI, D/607/A/539).
65 *The Press*, 14 Nov. 1797
66 Thomas Pelham to Mr Chevy, 31 March 1797 (PRONI, D/607/E/241).
67 Revd William Lambart to Thomas Pelham, 20 July 1797 (NAI, Reb. pap., 620/31/291).
68 Ibid.
69 Shawe Cartland to Edward Cooke, 10 July 1797 (NAI, Reb. pap., 620/28/250).
70 Shawe Cartland to Thomas Pelham, 21 May 1797 (NAI, Reb. pap., 620/30/132).
71 Revd William Lambart to Thomas Pelham, 20 July 1797 (NAI, Reb. pap. 620/31/291).
72 William Evans to Thomas Pelham, 26 September 1797 (NAI, Reb. pap., 620/32/143).
73 Thomas Dames to Thomas Pelham, 26 April 1797 (NAI, Reb. pap., 620/29/316).
74 John Everard to Thomas Pelham, 11 May 1797 (NAI, Reb. pap., 620/30/55).
75 John Pollock to Edward Cooke, 30 Aug. 1797 (NAI, Reb. pap., 620/32/89).
76 Robert Day to Edward Cooke, 19 Aug. 1797 (NAI, Reb. pap., 620/34/14).
77 John Pollock to Edward Cooke, 30 Aug. 1797 (NAI, Reb. pap., 620/32/89).
78 Ibid.
79 John Pomeroy to Viscount Harberton, May 1797 (PRONI, Harb. pap., T2954/8/13).
80 Lord Downshire to Edward Cooke, 9 December 1797 (NAI, Reb. pap., 620/33/135
81 Ibid.
82 Ibid.
83 *The Press*, 29 October 1797.

4. THE 1798 REBELLION:
EDENDERRY'S PART

1 Liam Chambers, 'The 1798 rebellion
in north Leinster' p. 127.
2 Jeanne Bulfin Winder, '1798 and 1803
rebellions' in Brian Pey (ed.), *Eglish
and Drumcullen, a parish in Firceall* (Birr,
2002), p. 98.
3 Thomas Bartlett, Kevin Dawson and
Dáire Keogh (eds), *Rebellion: a television
history of 1798* (Dublin, 1998), p. 86.
4 Robert Ross to Lord Downshire, 6
April 1798 (PRONI, D/607/F/131A).
5 R. B. McDowell, *Ireland in the age of
imperialism and revolution, 1760–1801*
(Oxford, 1979), p. 577
6 Ruán O'Donnell, 'Kings County in
1798' in Nolan & O'Neill (eds), *Offaly:
history and society*, p. 494.
7 Ibid.
8 John Wakely, Thomas Dames and Revd
William Lambart (magistrates in King's
County) to Edward Cooke, 21 April
1798 (NAI, Reb. pap., 620/36/193).
9 *Saunder's Newsletter*, 26 April 1797.
10 Robert Ross to Lord Downshire, 25
April 1798 (PRONI, D/607/F/150).
11 General Dunne to Lord Castlereagh,
31 July 1798 (NAI, Reb. pap.,
620/4/33/6).
12 Samuel Sproules to General Lee, 25
May 1798 (NAI, Reb. pap.,
620/51/200).
13 Richard Musgrave, *Memoirs of the
different rebellions in Ireland* (Dublin,
1801), p. 310.
14 Mrs Spenser to Viscount Harberton, 24
May 1798 (PRONI, Harb. pap.,
T/2954/8/16).
15 Confession of Stephen Hyland of New
Chapel in the Co. Kildare (blacksmith),
(NAI, Reb. pap., 620/30/47).
16 Mario Corrigan, *All that delirium of the
brave: Kildare in 1798* (Kildare, 1998),
p.87.
17 Musgrave, *Memoirs of the different
rebellions*, p. 309.
18 Ibid.
19 Ibid.
20 Lt-Col. Longfield to Lord Castlereagh,
29 May 1798 (NAI, Reb. pap.,
620/37/208).
21 Col. E. Dunne to Lt-Gen. Lake, 27
May 1798 (NAI, Reb. pap.,
620/37/209).
22 Ibid.
23 Ibid.
24 Ibid.
25 Ibid.
26 Stephen Sparks to Thomas Pelham, 10
Sept. 1797 (NAI, Reb. pap.,
620/32/108).
27 Ibid.
28 Ruán O'Donnell, 'King's County in
1798', *Offaly: history and society*, p. 501;
see also Karina Holton, 'Carbury, Co.
Kildare' in Liam Clare, Karina Holton
and Brian O'Dálaigh (eds), *Irish
villages: a study in local history* (Dublin,
2004), p. 123.
29 William Evans to Dublin Castle, June
1798 (NAI, Reb. Pap., 620/52/99).
30 Musgrave, *Memoirs of the different
rebellions*, p. 249.
31 John Jones, *An impartial narrative of each
engagement which took place between his
majesties forces and the rebels during the
Irish rebellion 1798* (Dublin, 1800), p. 9.
32 Ibid.
33 Pádraig Mac Suibhne, *Kildare in 98*
(Naas, 1978), p. 199.
34 Marquis of Downshire to Edward
Cooke, 23 June 1798 (NAI, Reb. pap.,
620/38/283).
35 O'Donnell, 'King's County in 1798', p.
502.
36 John Ormsby to Viscount Castlereagh,
1 July 1798 (MS letter in the
possession of the O'Connor family of
Clonuff, Broadford, Co. Kildare).
37 Ibid.
38 Ibid.
39 O'Donnell, 'King's County in 1798', p.
490.
40 Kieran Kennedy, 'The Limerick City
Militia 1798', in *Old Limerick Journal*
1966.
41 Captain Gough to Colonel Verecher,
12 July 1798 (NAI, Reb. pap.,
620/4/36/1).
42 John Ormsby to Viscount Castlereagh,
1 July 1798 (MS original letter in
the possession of the O'Connor
family of Clonuff, Broadford, Co.
Kildare).

43 William Hartigan to Lord Downshire, 6 July 1798 (PRONI, D/607/F/302).

44 McDowell, *Ireland in the age of imperialism and revolution, 1760–1801*, p. 635.

45 Eamon Doyle, *March into Meath* (Enniscorthy, 1998), p. 7.

46 Daniel Gahan, *The people's rising: Wexford 1798* (Dublin, 1995), p.284.

47 *Dublin Gazette*, 16 July 1798.

48 William Hartigan to Lord Downshire, 12 July 1798 (PRONI, D/607/F/315).

49 Peter O'Shaughnessy (ed.), *Rebellion in Wicklow: General Joseph Holt's personal account of 1798* (Dublin, 1998), p. 49.

50 Brian Ford to Viscount Harberton, 14 July 1798 (NAI, Reb. pap., 620/4/33/1).

51 Ibid.

52 Col. Gough to Col. Verecker, 12 July 1798 (NAI, Reb. pap., 620/4/36/1).

53 Ibid.

54 Ibid.

55 John Jones, *An impartial narrative of each engagement which took place between his majesties forces and the rebels during the Irish rebellion of 1798* (Dublin, 1800), p. 31.

56 O'Shaughnessy (ed.), *Rebellion in Wicklow*, p. 49.

57 John Cullen and Bill Murray (eds), *Epitaph of 1798: a photographic record of 1798 memorials in Ireland and beyond* (Enniscorthy, 2002), p. 115.

58 Thomas Pakenham, *The year of liberty: the history of the great Irish rebellion of 1798* (London, 1969), p. 327.

59 *Dublin Evening Post*, 20 Sept. 1798.

60 Patrick Power, *The court martials of 1798–99* (Kilkenny, 1997), pp 65–7.

61 Ibid.

62 NAI, Transportation Files (PPC 197).

63 Holton, 'Carbury, Co. Kildare', p. 123.

64 Douglas Glynn, *Friends and 1798*, pp 34–5.

65 Mairead Evans and Noel Whelan (eds), *Edenderry through the ages* (Edenderry, 2000), p. 32.

66 Pilkington Homan to Lord Downshire, 2 Sept. 1798 (PRONI, D/607/A/561).

67 Shawe Cartland to Lord Downshire, 9 Dec. 1798 (PRONI, D/607/A/572).

68 John Brownrigg to Capt. Taylor, 26 Dec. 1798 (PRONI, D/607/A/573).

69 Capt. Littlehales to John Brownrigg, 3 Jan. 1798 (PRONI, D/607/A/575).

70 William Evans to Edward Cooke, Sept. 1798 (NAI, Reb. pap., 620/52/99).

71 Francis Synge to Lord Downshire, 10 Oct. 1797 (PRONI, D/607/A/540).

72 Francis Synge to Lord Downshire, 7 Oct. 1797 (PRONI, D/607/A/539).

73 James Moorhead to Lord Downshire, 17 Dece. 1797 (PRONI, D/607/A/544b).

74 James Mooney to Lord Downshire, 6 March 1798 (PRONI, D/607/A/552).

75 Francis Synge to Miss Blundell, 14 June 1798 (PRONI, D/607/A/557).

76 Ibid.

77 Kathy Trant, *The Blessington estate, 1607–1908* (Dublin, 2004), p. 63.

78 George Stephenson to Lord Downshire, 10 June 1798 (PRONI, D/607/F/274).

79 Thomas Lane to Lord Downshire, 3 July 1798 (PRONI, D/607/F/298).

80 John Stephens to John Brownrigg, 31 Oct. 1798 (PRONI, D/607/A/567).

81 John Robinson to Lord Downshire, 18 Oct. 1798 (PRONI, D/607/A/563).

82 Ian Cantwell (ed.), *The 1798 rebellion: claimants and surrenders* (CD-ROM, Dublin: Eneclann, 2005).

83 Ibid.

5. AFTERMATH: COURTS MARTIAL AND POVERTY

1 John Gough, *Account of two journies southward in Ireland in 1817* (Dublin, 1817), p. 46.

2 Ibid.

3 Charles Coote, *Statistical survey of King's County* (Dublin, 1801), p. 121.

4 John Brownrigg to Captain Evans, 13 Dec. 1799 (Berkshire Record Office, MIC/17/1/290).

5 Ibid.

6 John Brownrigg to John Reilly, 12 March 1799 (PRONI, D/607/A/578).

7 John Brownrigg to Captain Evans, 13 Dec. 1799 (Berkshire Record Office, MIC/17/1/290).

8 John Brownrigg to Lord Downshire, 10 June 1800 (PRONI, D/607/A/604).

9 McDowell, *Ireland in the age of imperialism and revolution, 1760–1801* (Oxford, 1979), p. 673.

10 *The Times*, 21 Oct. 1799.

11 *The Times*, 30 May 1799.

12 Gilbert (ed.), *Documents relating to Ireland, 1795–1804*, p. 39.

13 John Brownrigg to Lord Downshire, 10 June 1800 (PRONI, D/607/A/604).

14 *The Times*, 28 August 1800.

15 Court Martials in King's County, 14 March 1800 (NAI, Reb. pap., 620/9/88).

16 Ibid.

17 NAI, Transportation papers (PPC 301).

18 Court Martial of Edward Allen and Michael Costello, 5 February 1800 (NAI, Reb. pap., 620/9/88).

19 Court Martials in King's County, 6 February 1800 (NAI, Reb. pap., 620/9/22).

20 Ruán O'Donnell, 'King's County in 1798' in Nolan & O'Neill (eds), *Offaly: history and society* (Dublin, 1998), p. 510.

21 Inhabitants of Philipstown, in King's County to Dublin Castle, 13 June 1800 (NAI, Reb. pap., 620/58/68).

22 Ibid.

23 Glynn, *Friends and 1798*, p. 36.

24 Charles Coote, *Statistical survey of King's County* (Dublin, 1801), p. 122.

25 Ibid.

26 John Brownrigg to Lord Downshire, 24 Sept. 1800 (PRONI, D/607/A/614).

27 John Brownrigg to Lord Downshire, 13 July 1800 (PRONI, D/607/A/605).

28 Lord Downshire to John Brownrigg, 13 Aug. 1800 (PRONI, D/607/A/608).

29 Lord Downshire to John Brownrigg, 12 March 1800 (PRONI, D/A/593).

30 Lord Downshire to John Brownrigg, 10 Dec. 1799 (PRONI, D/607/A/584).

31 Laura A. Martin, 'The Irish landed estate agent as a mediator of urban improvement at Banbridge, Co. Down,

and Edenderry, King's County, 1790–1840' (BSc thesis, University of Ulster, Coleraine, 1994).

32 James Brownrigg to Lord Downshire, 2 Aug. 1800 (PRONI, D/607/A/607).

33 Lord Downshire to John Brownrigg, 4 Jan. 1800 (PRONI, D/607/A/588).

34 Ibid.

35 James Brownrigg to Lord Downshire, 20 Jan. 1801 (PRONI, D/607/A/625).

36 The survey of Messrs J and D Busby mineral surveyors 1806 (PRONI, D/607/C/45/156).

37 Lord Downshire to John Brownrigg, 4 Jan. 1800 (PRONI, D/607/A/588).

38 Lord Downshire to John Brownrigg, 19 Jan. 1800 (PRONI, D/607/A/591).

39 *A letter from Darby Tracy, chairman in London, to Denis Feagan, breaches maker at Edenderry, where is clearly proved the effects which a union with Great Britain will have on the interests and happenings of the common people of Ireland* (Dublin, 1799).

40 Lord Downshire to James Brownrigg, 4 Jan. 1800 (PRONI, D/607/A/588).

41 James Brownrigg to Lord Downshire, 21 Aug. 1800 (PRONI, D/607/A/611).

42 Ibid.

43 Ibid.

44 Ibid.

45 Lord Downshire to James Brownrigg, 25 Dec. 1800 (PRONI, D/607/A/620).

46 Lord Downshire to James Brownrigg, 1 Sept. 1801 (PRONI, D/607/A/636).

47 James Brownrigg to Lord Downshire, 24 Aug. 1800 (PRONI, D/607/A/614).

6. CONCLUSION: MYTH, LEGEND AND COMMEMORATION

1 Tom Dunne, *Rebellions, memoir, memory and 1798* (Dublin, 2004), p. 3.

2 Noel Whelan, Address at the bicentenary celebrations at the grave of Mogue Kearns and Anthony Perry, 21 July 1999 (MS at Edenderry Public Library).

3 Ibid.
4 *King's County Chronicle*, 23 July 1898.
5 *Midland Tribune*, 23 July 1898.
6 Ibid.
7 *Leinster Leader*, 23 May 1898.
8 R.R. Madden (ed.), *Literary remains of the United Irishmen of 1798* (Dublin, 1887), pp 31–5, 170–3.
9 *King's County Chronicle*, 28 March 1908.
10 Edenderry Historical Society, *Edenderry welcomes President Mary Robinson to Edenderry, 15 June 1994* (Edenderry, 1994).
11 *Offaly Topic*, 27 June 1986.
12 Edenderry Historical Society, *Local lore and legends of 1798 commemorative pamphlet* (Edenderry, 1998).
13 Ibid.
14 *The Standard*, August 1953 (MS at Edenderry Public Library).
15 *Leinster Express*, 28 November 1983
16 O'Shaugnessy (ed.), *Rebellion in Wicklow.*
17 Peter O'Shaughnessy (ed.), *A rum story: adventures of Joseph Holt* (Sydney, 1988).
18 John Brownrigg to Lord Downshire, 24 Sept. 1800 (PRONI, D/607/A/614).